HOME **CHARCUTERIE**

HOME CHARCUTERIE

Make your own bacon, sausages, salami and other cured meats

Paul Thomas

LORENZ BOOKS

CONTENTS

INTRODUCTION

Other than attempting to cure some salmon or turning out a pâté occasionally, my first real interest in charcuterie came when I was working as a farmhouse cheesemaker. Someone was keeping pigs nearby and was using the whey, which is a by-product of cheesemaking, to feed them. Whey-fed pork has an incredibly sweet flavour, and I could not pass up the opportunity to buy half a pig when it was offered. With limited space to freeze the meat, it was not long before I started experimenting with curing it instead.

Charcuterie as a term describes the preparation of meat products such as bacon, ham, sausages and pâté. Some of these products are cooked during their preparation, however many others are cured, which means that they are preserved by salting or drying. Many of these techniques have been carried out over hundreds or even thousands of years and arose from the necessity to preserve meat in the days before freezers and refrigerators.

In this book, I will cover techniques for some of the most well-known cured pork and beef products, ranging from home-cured bacon to air-dried ham. I will demonstrate the preparation of cooked meat products such as confit duck and cooked ham, and we will explore the basic principles of smoking cuts of meat and fish. As it is an old favourite, I have also included the recipe for gravadlax, which is salmon cured in dill, salt and sugar.

The recipes are easy to follow and, in many cases, do not require special equipment or a great deal of experience. All that is needed is the ability to follow the instructions, weigh out the ingredients carefully, and have some patience while the meats cure. This is an almost magical process and one to be enjoyed.

Before beginning any of the recipes I do recommend that you read the guidance notes in the first chapters of the book as they give clear instructions on how to follow the processes safely. They describe the main food safety hazards relevant to cured meat and fish, and show how these can be controlled. If you follow some simple rules the risk of failure is low. In the many years that I have been curing meat I have only had one significant failure; some flies managed to find their way into the meat safe that held a leg of pork. It was a disappointment, of course, but it pales into insignificance in comparison to all of the times when I have enjoyed carving and eating the many and various cured meats that I have made. Charcuterie production and cheesemaking share something in common; both contain elements of science wrapped up in a coat of magic. There is something incredibly satisfying about presenting a platter of your own charcuterie products, or a dish prepared from them, to the amazement of your guests.

PAUL THOMAS

1

BASICS

This chapter covers all of the essential information that you need to know before starting any of the recipes. Here, you will find important advice on sourcing and storing raw materials, including meat, salt, starters, casings and curing salts. The type of equipment used in the book is covered in detail and there are some key notes on food safety to ensure that the products made are both delicious and safe to eat.

THE RAW INGREDIENTS

The economics of curing your own meat makes sense, as the cost of raw meat as an ingredient is a fraction of what it would cost to buy the same meat once it had been cured and sliced. Nonetheless it makes sense to buy the highest possible quality in raw materials and ingredients.

MEAT

Pork, beef or venison are commonly used as raw materials in the creation of cured meat products. Whichever species is used, it is important that the slaughter and butchery of the animal are carried out under the strictest hygiene conditions and the meat is refrigerated before processing. It should be as fresh as possible, especially where the meat is to be cured and dried without heat treatment.

Minced or ground meat used to produce salami should not be bought ready-minced. Buy whole cuts of meat and grind them yourself immediately before making salami. Read the section on food safety on pages 34–35 before attempting any of the recipes.

Chicken is not suitable for the preparation of cured but uncooked charcuterie products.

FISH

Several species of fish are used for the preparation of cured fish products. The recipes described in this book use salmon and herring. Other types of fish, such as cod, may also be preserved by salting.

Always buy fish that is very fresh. The eyes should be bright rather than dark, bloody or sunken. The flesh is usually firm when fresh, and strong fishy smells can indicate spoilage. Observe the food safety instructions on pages 34–35 to avoid the risk of parasitic infection. The processes in the chapter on curing and smoking are easy and safe, so long as the simple steps are followed.

CASINGS

Casings are the natural or artificial outers which are used to prepare salamis and some other air-dried products as well as cooked sausages. They are also used in the preparation of haggis.

Natural casings are prepared from the cleaned and de-slimed intestines of pigs or ruminant animals. The 'slime' is a mucosal layer of the intestines. Hog, beef and sheep casings are widely available from specialist butchery suppliers. The casings are packed in salt to preserve them and must be soaked for a couple of hours before use. The small intestines are usually used for sausages where the casing will be eaten, whereas bungs and middles are not edible. Natural casings which are soaked but not used may be salted again,

OPPOSITE 1 Clockwise from left: Pork cheeks, back fat, pork shoulder or boston butt, ribs and pork belly, leg of pork, fillet or tenderloin **2** Clockwise from left: hog middles, beef bung, fibrous casings, hog casings

BASICS

with ordinary table salt, and stored for future use. Natural casings should not be frozen as this can reduce their elasticity and may lead to damage which increases the risk of splitting.

Artificial, or manufactured, 'fibrous' casings made from cellulose are also available, as are those derived from animal collagen or synthetic casings made from thermoplastics including polyethylene (PE), polypropylene (PP), polyamide (PA) and polyvinyldenchloride (PVDC). Synthetic casings are not suitable for fermented or dried products.

Collagen casings are sometimes used for sausages, but those with a diameter wider than 3cm/1in are not usually edible and may be peeled off. Unlike natural casings, artificial casings come in standardised diameters. Cellulose and collagen casings are most commonly available to the home charcutier.

Beef casings Beef rounds or runners are the small intestines of cattle, with a diameter of 3–5cm/1–2in. Beef bungs are the caecum of cattle, with a diameter of 7–10cm/2¾–4in, and can be used for haggis and large salami. Beef middles are the large intestines of cattle with a diameter of 4–7cm/1½–2¾in, drying to half that diameter. They can be used for salami.

Hog casings Made from the small intestine, hog casings have a diameter of 3–4cm/1–1½in and are suitable for a wide variety of fresh sausages and small, cured products such as pepperoni. They are usually sold by the hank, half-hank or quarter-hank. A hank refers to a coil or bundle rather than a fixed weight but is usually around 90 metres/98 yards long. Hog middles, or 'chitterlings', are used for dried salami and black pudding.

Sheep casings Made from the small intestine, sheep casings have a diameter of just under 2–3cm/¾–1in and are suitable for fresh sausages. Handle them carefully; they can be quite delicate and are prone to splitting if overfilled, but they make for a pleasant texture and mouthfeel in the finished sausage.

Fibrous cellulose and collagen casings Cellulose is an organic polymer, often derived from cotton or wood. Wider-diameter fibrous casings made of reinforced cellulose are available and can be suitable for large salami. This casing is not edible and is peeled off prior to slicing the salami.

Collagen casings are made from dried beef protein. Like cellulose casings they can be easy to fill without bursting, though they can lack the elasticity of natural casings and it can be more difficult to exclude the air from them.

These casings come in a variety of standard sizes: the cellulose casings are available with a diameter of 7–8cm/2¾–3in and the collagen products start at around 2–3cm/¾–1in.

STARTER CULTURES

Available to buy as sachets of freeze-dried powder or granules, starter cultures are typically a mixture of lactic acid bacteria and other ripening organisms such as *Staphylococcus xylosus*. These starters are used in the production of salami and so-called 'live' brines such as that used for the Wiltshire cure. They have an important bio-protective effect as they can compete against harmful or less desirable bacteria in the meat during the fermentation, maturation and storage processes.

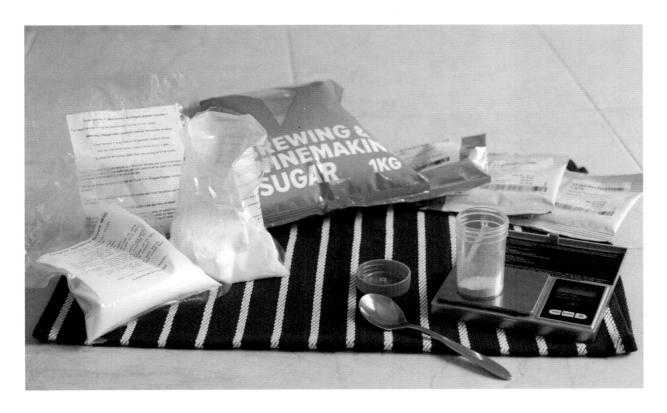

ABOVE The key ingredients and equipment for making salami, clockwise from left: curing salts, dextrose, starter cultures, and a set of scales to weigh small quantities of the cultures

The activity of the starters can reduce the pH of the meat, creating a less favourable environment for the growth of harmful bacteria. This is an important controlling factor in the safety of salami; however, as the fermentation conditions of salt and temperature must also be suitable for the growth of the starter bacteria, it is important to follow the recipe or manufacturer's instructions precisely.

The starter culture can also have an important role in the development of the flavour of cured meats, and also in the pigmentation through the conversion of nitrate into compounds which 'fix' the naturally red colour of meat.

Store starter cultures in the freezer unless the manufacturer's instructions indicate otherwise. For best results, decant any unused starter into a sealed plastic pot to keep it dry during storage. The starter may be used after the best-before date, however its activity may become impaired over time, particularly when it has not been carefully stored, and you should discard any culture which appears damp, starts to clump, or sticks to the sides of the packaging.

The following examples described overleaf are three of the more commonly available starter cultures typically used in the preparation of fermented meat products.

Bitec LS25 A rapid acidifying culture consisting of *Staphylococcus carnosus* and *Lactobacillus sakei*. The culture is intended to be used to make fermented sausages, with curing salt. This culture is able to ferment dextrose and sucrose. Its rapid acidifying cultures produce fermented meat products with a tangy flavour. The typical dose is 0.25g/¹/₁₆oz of culture per 1kg (2.2lb) of meat. It should be dissolved in cold water before being added to the minced or ground meat.

Christian Hansen F-LC SafePro An acidifying culture consisting of *Staphylococcus xylosus*, *Lactobacillus curvatus* and *Pediococcus acidilactici*, this is used in the production of traditional slow-fermented salami, and ensures effective inhibition of *Listeria*. This culture is able to ferment glucose/dextrose and sucrose. The typical dose is 0.25g/¹/₁₆oz of culture per 1kg (2.2lb) of meat, and it is added directly to the minced or ground meat. A minimum temperature of 15°C/59°F is required to ensure the growth of all three species in this culture.

T-SPX Bactoferm An acidifying culture consisting of *Staphylococcus xylosus* and *Pediococcus pentosaceus*, this is used in the production of traditional slow-fermented salami. This culture can ferment dextrose/glucose and sucrose. The typical dose is 0.13g of culture per 1kg (2.2lb) of meat, and the fermentation may be carried out between 18–24°C/64–75°F.

OPPOSITE Hams are packed in salt for several days in order to cure the meat before air-drying

SALT

Pure Dried Vacuum (PDV) Salt Common salt or sodium chloride is a key ingredient in the preparation of cured meat and fish. Pure dried vacuum (PDV) is called for in many of the recipes. This is the same as ordinary free-flowing table salt and the name simply refers to the process by which the salt is dried under a vacuum. In countries where iodine is routinely added, iodinised salt should be avoided as it can inhibit some of the microorganisms necessary for the safe preparation of cured foods, but there is no issue with the presence of anti-caking agents in the salt.

The principal role of salt is to make water inaccessible to harmful bacteria. It also draws some of the water out of the meat at the start of the curing process, then begins to migrate into the middle of the meat being cured.

The salt can only dissolve in the water which is present, not the fat or protein. For this reason, the salt in moisture or 'aqueous salt' measure gives a more realistic impression of the effect that the salt has than the percentage of salt which is present. Aqueous salt is calculated by multiplying the percentage of salt by 100 and then dividing it by the sum of percentage salt and percentage moisture. Meat with a moisture content of 75% which takes up 5% salt will have an aqueous salt of 6.25%, effectively concentrating the salt into the portion of the meat in which harmful bacteria might otherwise be able to grow.

Because of the significant role that salt has in controlling the safety of cured products, it is not a good idea to reduce salt or to substitute it with sodium-replacement salt which may contain a higher proportion of potassium chloride or magnesium chloride. These salts would not have the same protective effect and may allow for the growth of very harmful bacteria.

Salt suitable for curing should be free-flowing or present in fine crystals to ensure that it is easily adsorbed. Where salt uptake is slow, it may compromise safety. I usually use pure dried vacuum salt to cure most meat products, though I have used fleur de sel, or the sea salt which is evaporated in the English town of Maldon. These have very delicate, beautiful irregular crystals which dissolve easily. I do not use coarse salt and as a matter of preference, I would try to source local rather than exotic imported salts such as Himalayan pink salt.

As already mentioned, iodised salt may inhibit the activity of microbes present in the starter cultures, and iodised salt should not be used to cure meat.

To calculate the exact quantity of salt, divide your actual meat weight into the weight specified in the recipe then multiply the resulting number by the salt weight specified in the recipe. So: adjusted salt = actual weight of meat x weight of salt in recipe / weight of meat in recipe. For example: 1.25kg/2¾lb actual meat x 100g/3½oz salt in recipe divided by 1kg/2.2lb meat in recipe = 125g/2¾oz adjusted salt.

CURING SALTS

While cured meats certainly need common salt, there is some controversy over the subject of curing salts. Sodium nitrate and sodium nitrite are commonly used as curing salts, and have a preservative antimicrobial effect, inhibiting the growth of *Clostridium botulinum*. There are examples of nitrate-free cured meats and the use of nitrate has

OPPOSITE Curing salts are toxic and they must be weighed accurately, at a dose appropriate to the quantity of trimmed meat

been banned for manufacturing some products for many years. The controversy over use of the salts relates to concerns over their toxicity and cancer-promoting properties. We must therefore weigh up these risks against a very real risk posed by harmful bacteria, particularly where the source of the raw materials and the hygiene involved in their production are not tightly controlled by the person curing the meat.

Those traditional cured foods which avoid the use of nitrate often also involve well-established and controlled standards of primary production, which may have been in operation for many years. Nonetheless, while it may be possible to make nitrate-free cured meat, it is not safe to assume that the quality controls producing apparently similar raw ingredients are always there, when the primary produce could be made under different circumstances, in a different geographical location, with very different standards. Where curing salts are not used, very careful control of other manufacturing parameters must be achieved, including knowledge of the hygienic quality of the raw materials, strict temperature control, and monitoring of the satisfactory growth of a protective microflora.

The two Cures or Prague Powders that follow are commonly used in the preparation of cured meat products. Do not use curing salts as a replacement for ordinary salt, and they should not be used in quantities higher than specified by the manufacturer.

If curing salts are used, weigh out very carefully and mix well into the PDV salt for an even distribution. Curing salts are toxic if the dose is exceeded

Curing Salt #1 Also known as Prague Powder 1 or Cure #1, this contains 6.25% sodium nitrite and 93.75% salt. It is used in small quantities, in addition to ordinary salt, for products such as bacon which will be cooked before serving. It is typically used at a dose of 2.5g per 1 kg (2.2lb) of trimmed meat but follow the manufacturer's instructions exactly.

Curing Salt #2 Also known as Prague Powder 2 or Cure #2, this contains 6.25% sodium nitrite, 4% sodium nitrate and 89.75% salt. It is used in small quantities, in addition to ordinary salt, for meat products which are not cooked before serving, such as air-dried meats and salami. It is typically used at a dose of 2.5g per 1 kg (2.2lb) of trimmed meat but the manufacturer's instructions must be followed exactly.

SUGAR

Sugars such as sucrose (common table sugar) or glucose (dextrose powder) are often added to salami mixes. They act as food for the starter cultures which convert the sugars into lactic acid, lowering the pH of the meat. This can inhibit the growth of harmful bacteria and impart a tangy sour flavour to the salami.

Always check that the sugar is the right kind to be fermented by the starter culture you have. The starter supplier will have this information. It is no good using sucrose with a starter culture that ferments glucose but not sucrose. Other sugars may work, but artificial sweeteners should not be used.

HERBS AND SPICES

The following herbs and spices are commonly used in the preparation of cured meat products. When following some of the recipes in this book, it can be interesting to experiment to create alternative blends for cured meats, salamis and cooked sausages.

Allspice Also called Jamaican pepper, this is the fruit of a plant which is native to Central America. The dried fruit has gently warming flavours reminiscent of cloves or nutmeg. It is used in Jamaican jerk seasoning and can make an interesting addition to sausage mixes. Use it in small quantities as it has a strong flavour.

Cinnamon This is the dried and rolled inner bark of the Cinnamomum tree, which is native to South East Asia. The flavour is sweet and spicy, adding extra complexity to sausage and cured salami mixes.

Cayenne pepper and chilli powder Cayenne is the fruit of a hot pepper of the genus Capsicum. There are many different varieties, depending on the strength of the pepper used to prepare it, measured on the Scoville Pepper Scale. Chilli powder is a blend of cayenne pepper and paprika and its strength may also vary depending on the blend.

Cloves The dried brown flowerheads of an evergreen tree found in Indonesia, India and Madagascar, cloves have a pungent bittersweet flavour which can have a numbing effect when chewed. Used sparingly, they add complexity to brine-cured or air-dried meats and can be used to decorate a baked ham.

Coriander and cilantro The dried seeds of the coriander plant have a strong citrus flavour and impart orange and lemon notes to biltong and boerewors. The leaves of the plant (coriander leaves or cilantro) can also be used in cooking, providing a milder flavour.

Cumin A small green-brown seed found in the Middle East. Often used alongside other spices, it has a gentle heat and slight bitterness. A small amount can add complexity to the flavour.

Dill Both the fresh leaves and the dried seeds of the plant are used. It is commonly encountered in the cooking of Russia and the Scandinavian countries. Dill has a gentle anise-flavour, like caraway, and is a classic ingredient in the preparation of gravadlax.

Fennel Native to the Mediterranean counties, the stem of the fennel plant can be used, or the small oval seeds which are dried to give a savoury anise-like flavour. Fennel works well with cured salami mixes.

Garlic A member of the allium or onion family, with a pungent and lingering flavour. The cloves of the garlic bulb can be used fresh or are available as a powder. Both are suitable for air-dried meats and salamis. The leaves of the young plant can also be used, and these have a milder flavour and can make an interesting addition to sausage mixes.

RIGHT Freshly chopped, dill imparts an aniseed-flavour to gravadlax and is also used in the sauce used to dress the fish

Mustard seeds The yellow/white or black/brown seed of one of several plants of the genus Brassica, with a hot and pungent flavour. The flavour of the yellow or white mustard is usually milder. Mustard seeds may make part of the spice mix for sausages and salamis but of course are also used with vinegar to prepare the well-known paste of the same name, which can be used to glaze ham, and which has a natural affinity with beef.

Nutmeg and mace Nutmeg is the brown dried seed of a tree which originated in Indonesia. Mace is the dried covering of the nutmeg seed. Both have a pleasantly sweet flavour and gentle warmth. They have a natural affinity with cured meats including salami mixes using pork.

Paprika The dried fruit of a member of the Capsicum or pepper family that is native to the Americas. A mild slightly sweet pepper flavour, with less heat than cayenne pepper, paprika comes in a variety of strengths, with dolce being the lightest. Smoked versions are also available, such as the Pimenton dolce used to flavour lomo, a Spanish cured pork fillet.

Black and white pepper Black pepper is the cooked and dried unripe fruit of the Piper nigrum plant, native to Asia. It is widely used in a variety of cured meat products and used as a table seasoning. It has a savoury taste, a pungent smell and some heat. White pepper is the ripe fruit of the same plant, which is soaked to remove the outer husk. Black pepper is more aromatic, while white pepper has more heat. The whole peppercorns are sometimes used in dried salami, whereas the ground pepper is more often used to flavour a wide range of cured meats.

Rosemary A woody perennial plant originating in the Mediterranean. The leaves are used, either dried or fresh. The leaves have a bitter flavour and a pungent and slightly medicinal aroma. Use sparingly to avoid it overpowering the flavour of a cured meat. Rosemary works well when used to flavour air-dried whole cuts, but is perhaps too tough to use in salami where it would be eaten.

OPPOSITE 1 Whole juniper berries **2** Fennel seeds **3** Coriander seeds **4** Ground cinnamon **5** Star anise **6** Salt **7** Ground ginger **8** Garlic powder

Sumac The powdered dried berry of the Rhus plant, used extensively in Middle Eastern cookery. The dark red powder has a pleasant lemony flavour and works well with lamb and beef.

Thyme and oregano Thyme is closely related to oregano and marjoram. The leaves are used in cooking, either dried or fresh, and they are common ingredients in cured salami and sausage mixes. The flavours are warm and aromatic. With salt, sumac and sesame seeds they are an ingredient in the Middle Eastern spice mixture za'atar, often served with flatbreads and oil, or used as a seasoning for lamb.

Star anise This is the seed-containing pericarp of a tree from South-east Asia. The seeds have an anise-like flavour. Star anise is one of the main ingredients in Chinese five spice along with cloves, cinnamon, fennel, and Szechuan pepper. The latter is a dried berry of a tree, unrelated to black or white pepper, and which has a numbing effect on the tongue; it is often used in conjunction with other flavours.

Ginger The rhizome of a plant native to Asia with a hot, slightly sweet flavour. Used sparingly, dried and powdered ginger can add complexity to a spice mix along with mace, nutmeg or anise-type flavours. It can make an interesting addition to sausage mixes and was a flavour frequently used in traditional English cooking.

Tarragon Widespread across Europe, Asia and North America, the fresh herb has a sweet, gentle anise-like flavour, and is often used in chicken and fish dishes.

EQUIPMENT

It is likely that the reader will already possess most of the equipment needed for many of the recipes in this book. Most cures can be attempted with a set of scales, some string, a good sharp knife, some plastic food bags, and a large plastic container. While they are generally not essential, it is possible to buy other reasonably inexpensive labour-saving devices, to help with mincing and stuffing sausages and salamis for example, or to make it easier to cut hams. These items are a useful addition to the kit list of anyone likely to make a lot of cured meat products at home.

MINCING & STUFFING

Mincer or grinder While those with enough time on their hands might choose to mince their meat by hand using a knife, it is more likely that a mincer of some description will be used to make the sausages and salami. There are a number of options available. At the cheapest end of the range a hand-cranked mincer, usually made of aluminium, steel or plastic, will make short work of small cuts of meat. These mincers often come with filling nozzles which will make it easier to stuff casings with small quantities of sausage and salami mixtures.

Some food processors have a special mincing attachment. It is also possible to use the standard blade attachment but this is a very imprecise method and is likely to turn the meat into a purée. Slightly better results can be achieved by cubing and then partially freezing the meat before cutting it.

Plastic funnel It is possible to use a wide funnel to stuff sausages manually though it can be difficult to do this neatly unless you have some help.

Hand-cranked sausage stuffer The more ambitious home charcutier may wish to invest in a stuffer. These are available in a variety of sizes suitable for anything from occasional use by the hobbyist right up to semi-professional salami production. Choose a stuffer which is easy to take apart and clean.

Combination mincer and stuffer If you plan on making a lot of sausages or salami then an entry-level combined mincer and stuffer will make the task a lot easier. These work in largely the same way as the manual mincers except they are automated, cutting down on the effort required. They are usually much bulkier though, taking up more space than their manual counterparts, and requiring some regular use to justify their place in the kitchen. Choose one which is easy to take apart and clean.

Butcher's string and netting A reel of natural butcher's string is necessary for tying some of the cured meats, and mesh netting is useful.

OPPOSITE 1 A hand-cranked mincer or grinder **2** A wide plastic funnel for stuffing sausages **3** A hand-cranked sausage stuffer **4** An electric stuffer and filler

1

2

3

4

CURING WITH SALT

While the term curing can refer to both the salting and drying of the meat, the uptake of salt is always carried out first. It has a critical role as a preservative in the preparation of many charcuterie products.

Refrigerator Most of the cured meat recipes described in this book require a period of time at temperatures of 3–5°C/37–41°F during the early part of the process, as the salt is slowly diffusing into the centre of the meat and it is still vulnerable to the growth of harmful bacteria. While these temperatures may traditionally have been achieved by ambient storage during some of the coldest months of the year, the home charcutier should use their refrigerator to achieve these temperatures consistently. A fridge thermometer may be useful to check the temperature during the curing process. Some cures and brines take up a lot of space, and you might find a separate small fridge is useful if you do a lot of home charcuterie.

Once cured meats are sliced, they should be kept in the fridge to maintain quality. Protect them from drying out with clingfilm or food wrap. To avoid the risk of cross-contamination, always keep raw and part-cured meats on a shelf below those which are fully cured, as well as below other ready-to-eat foods.

Access to a freezer will be necessary for freezing cuts of meat or fish before curing them (see 34–35).

OPPOSITE 1 A large plastic bucket makes a good brine tank **2** Curing can be carried out easily in large zip-lock bags or vacuum pouches **3** A small vacuum-packer, vacuum pouches, and roll of muslin

Brine tank A large food-grade plastic tub or bucket will be useful for brining larger cuts of meat. These tubs should be in good condition without cracks or surface abrasions which can harbour harmful bacteria. The brine will need to be kept cool during use, so you will need enough room in the refrigerator to hold the tank. Wash out the brine tank with hot soapy water before and after use but do not use abrasive sponges or scrubbers as these can damage the surface of the plastic.

Pots or pans made of reactive metals (such as aluminium and copper) are not suitable for brining meat as they will be attacked by the brine. Stainless steel pans are non-reactive but the brine can corrode the steel over prolonged periods.

Plastic bags Vacuum-pack plastic bags tend to be quite tough and are very useful for curing cuts of meat. They can be sealed by tying or clipping the ends of the bag and disposed of after use (do not fully vacuum-seal them during curing; see note below). An alternative is to use plastic zip-lock style freezer bags. Sandwich bags tend to be quite thin and prone to splitting so they are not always the best option.

Regardless of the type used, all plastic bags do sometimes leak so make sure that they are positioned safely in the refrigerator in such a way that they do not pose a contamination risk to other foods around and below them.

While fully cured dried meats should be suitable for vacuum-packing, meats should not be vacuum-sealed during the early part of curing, when the level of adsorbed salt may be too low to control the growth of pathogenic bacteria such as non-proteolytic *Clostridium botulinum*.

HANGING AND DRYING

Butcher's hooks and bacon comb A selection of hooks make it easy to hang cured meats. They come in a range of sizes but for most home charcutiers, the smaller will be sufficient. The hooks should be cleaned thoroughly before being used to skewer meat.

The bacon comb features a row of hooks mounted on a single bar. It is used to hang slightly larger or heavier cuts such as bacon or pancetta, which might otherwise become damaged if hung from a single hook for prolonged periods.

Meat safe A meat safe is a ventilated cupboard, usually free-standing and often made of wood, which allows cured meats to dry but which affords some protection from pests such as rodents or insects. At least some of the sides are made of gauze. The gauze can be made of plastic but should be made of metal if there is a possibility of rodents. The meat safe can be positioned indoors in a cool and draughty location but can also be left outdoors so long as it is watertight. The safe should be placed high enough that pests cannot easily access it.

There are plenty of vintage meat safes available second-hand on the internet, some in better condition than others. It is not a difficult to make a meat safe using an old cupboard or packing crate, simply by cutting a large hole in each of two sides,

OPPOSITE A plastic box makes a cheap fermentation chamber, protecting the salami from contamination while the starters complete the fermentation

and tacking gauze over the holes. A more ambitious carpenter may even choose to build their own.

While it is less romantic than a vintage meat safe, it is possible to make a simple safe using a large plastic crate covered with a cotton sheet secured with bungee cords to protect the contents from insects. This type of safe should only be used indoors as it will not offer sufficient protection from rodents.

Fermentation box For fermented meat products such as salami, it is sometimes necessary to keep them in a warm, slightly humid place, away from sources of contamination. The type of plastic crate described above can also make a low-cost fermentation box. Here the lid of the crate is used instead of a cotton sheet as the purpose of the box is to retain heat and humidity rather than to dry the meat. To hang the salami, a bar can be placed into the box (as pictured left) if two holes are drilled on either side. Cool the drill bit in the freezer before using to prevent burring of the plastic, and be careful not to press too hard when drilling as this can cause the plastic to crack.

Biltong box Some smaller dried meats, such as biltong and jerky, can be made with a reasonable degree of success in a food desiccator. The more committed might choose to use a 'biltong box'. This is a small cabinet, sometimes made of wood, with a lightbulb to provide heat and a small fan to gently circulate air. Traditionally, the meat would have been cured by leaving it to hang in dry conditions with a slight breeze; the box simulates these conditions. Alternatively, biltong can be made in an oven on a very low temperature and with the door left slightly ajar, as is done in the biltong recipe on page 220.

Hygrometer A small digital hygrometer can be very useful to monitor the relative humidity of the air as meats are drying. If humidity is too high then the meat can become mouldy, whereas if the air is too dry, the casing and outside of the meat can harden, making it more difficult for moisture to escape from the core. The optimum humidity might typically be around 70–80% during the drying period, possibly a little higher at the start and becoming drier later.

Without a humidity-controlled drying chamber, the amateur charcutier might need to be a little more creative in achieving the optimum conditions in home conditions. A hygrometer can be useful in identifying the level of ambient humidity, allowing the charcutier to pick the best location in which to dry cured meats.

Thermometer A small digital thermometer, accurate to 0.1 degree Celsius, is necessary for many of the recipes and should not be overlooked as the safety of many of the cured meats depends on satisfactory temperature control. I like waterproof thermometers such as the Comark PDQ400 as they are easy to clean and less likely to stop working after an accidental soaking.

pH papers or meter Because the safety of some of the fermented salamis depends on the growth of an acidifying culture, it will be necessary to monitor the acidity development during fermentation. This can be done with a small pH meter accurate to 0.1–0.2 point or some pH papers, which are less accurate but cheap and easy to use, the paper being pressed against the sample and the colour change on the strip being read against a chart to determine the pH value. A pH meter will also require some calibration buffers to ensure that it is accurate. Every pH meter is slightly different and has individual instructions so always follow the specific manufacturer's recommendations.

CUTTING AND SLICING

Knives Carving knives often resemble a chef's knife in shape but are usually thinner with less curvature to the blade. The tip may be rounded or pointed. They are used in a sawing rather than chopping motion.

Boning knives often have narrow pointed blades, which can be more flexible than other knives to allow them to get in around bones to separate them from the flesh. The blade may be straight or slightly curved and may come in a variety of different sizes. These knives are particularly useful for preparing primal cuts of meat for curing.

A sharpening steel is essential for keeping knives in perfect condition and should be used every time before the knife is used. For instructions on sharpening knives see overleaf. A sharpening stone, such as a Japanese Waterstone, can be used for the same purpose but it less practical for day-to-day sharpening than the steel.

While this book does not look at the butchery skills required to prepare the cuts of meat for curing and drying, those who want to butcher as well as preserve the meat will most likely need to add a bone saw and a large cleaver to their kit list.

OPPOSITE 1 A bone saw for cutting the raw meat **2** An electric meat slicer for slicing cured charcuterie; use with care and protective gloves

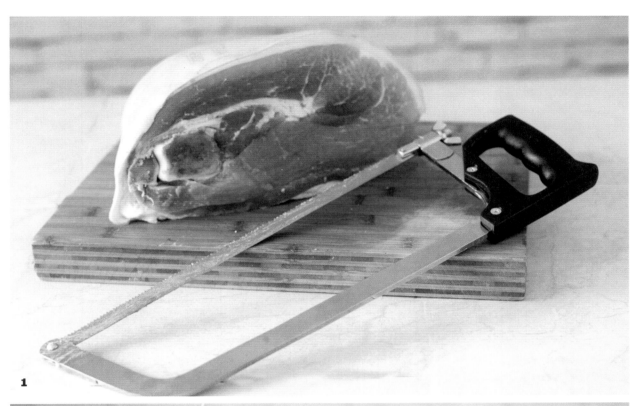

1

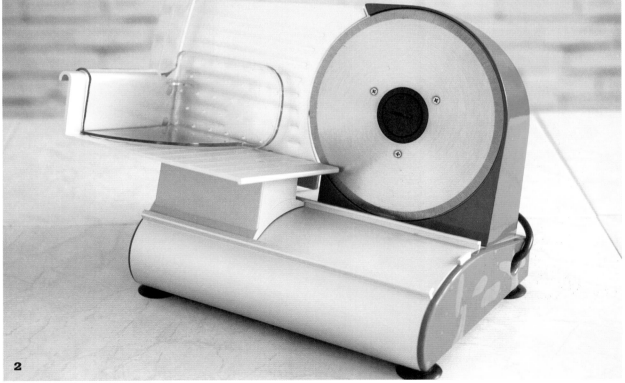

2

Meat slicer Small meat slicers are increasingly common and not overly expensive; they are often aimed at restaurateurs who want to cut salamis and cured meats to order. Such a slicer may be an unnecessary expense for most amateur charcutiers, who may prefer to cut by hand. Use a cut-resistant or chain-mail glove when using the slicer and keep your hands away from the moving blade.

Ham stand While it is possible to carve smaller cured meats by hand using only a knife, a jamonero or ham stand makes the job easier and safer when carving whole hams. These stands are a familiar sight across Spain; the thin foot end is clamped into position near the hock while the widest part of the ham is fixed on a spike to prevent it from moving around as fine slices are carved with an extremely sharp knife.

SHARPENING A KNIFE

Forget attempts at dramatic knife sharpening displays, the best way to keep your blades in tip-top condition is to relax your grip and let gravity do the hard work. Sharpen your knife every time before using it. The ability of the steel to sharpen knives will deteriorate over time. Replace the steel if it begins to feel smooth.

1 Stand the sharpening steel on a work surface. Place a towel underneath the steel to collect the fine metal filings that will be produced.

2 Hold the knife with a loose hand rather than a tight grip. Position the heel of the knife at the top of the sharpening steel at an angle of around 30°. The knife should be lightly touching the steel but should not be pressed against it.

3 Allowing gravity to do the hard work, let the knife glide gently against the steel, pulling it back as it does, to draw all parts of the blade across the sharpening steel. This should be a very slow and effortless action. Do not push the blade against the steel!

4 Repeat the sharpening action on the other side of the blade. Each side of the blade should be sharpened an equal number of times; about five times on each side should be enough to sharpen the knife.

SMOKING

Smoker A smoker is simply a 'box' of some description, which is able to retain smoke around a food long enough for the aroma to be adsorbed. At its simplest, it is possible to make a smoker from a large, double-walled cardboard box, which can then be broken up and composted after it has been used a few times or starts to fall apart.

A cold smoke generator, which is a small pan or tube typically filled with wood dust, may be a good idea to use with your box. This allows cold smoke, which is typically below 30°C/86°F, to be generated over several hours. Alternatively, the smoke source and the chamber should be separated by a few metres of pipe, so the smoke cools before it reaches the food.

For hot smoking, in which the temperature of the smoke is higher so that the food begins to cook, I often use a lidded 'barrel-type' barbecue grill in which food can cook in the heat of the smoke that is generated by the wood chips or briquettes.

While it is possible to buy a smoker or large kamado-style oven suitable for the job, I have seen a number of wonderful home-made smokers over the years, including ones that appeared to be built from found parts from an old wardrobe or cupboard, a garden shed, a metal filing cabinet, and even an old British red telephone box!

Wood chips A variety of different wood chips are available: oak is quite common but others include apple, cherry – which can impart sweet and subtle smokiness – and hickory, which provides a stronger-flavoured smoke.

It is possible to use your own wood to smoke but make sure that it has been dried over several months and is free from sap. Avoid coniferous woods such as pine, as well as any wood that has been treated with a preservative. Beech, birch, apple, cherry, pear, oak, hickory and maple are all fine. Also bear in mind that the smoke from some exotic timbers can contain harmful compounds, and these timbers should not be used to smoke food.

LEFT Lighting the wood chips and dust in a small smoker

OPPOSITE 1 A cold smoke generator is filled with wood dust **2** A tealight is used to ignite the wood dust **3** The lit dust burns slowly over several hours

HYGIENE & FOOD SAFETY

As when preparing any food which will not be cooked prior to serving, it is important to follow basic hygiene. Wash hands in hot water with soap, remembering to wash your thumbs, between the fingers, and to scrub palms and nails, before rinsing and drying on a clean towel. Wear clean clothes or an apron. Pets should be kept away from areas used to prepare food, and curing meats protected from pests such as insects, birds and rodents.

The equipment that is used to prepare food should be thoroughly washed in hot soapy water after use to remove grease and dirt. It should also be washed before use if it has not been used for a while.

Some items may be disinfected prior to use using a household disinfectant such as sodium hypochlorite (thin bleach). This is done to remove traces of harmful organisms which may remain on surfaces. Chemical disinfection is not suitable for some metal equipment including anything made of aluminium, but it is possible to use hot water to sterilise equipment instead. Note that where household disinfection is used, it will not be effective unless the equipment has been adequately cleaned beforehand.

While disinfection is commonplace in factories which produce food, it is less common in the home environment or among some producers of traditional foods. Effective washing of any equipment that is to be used can be very good at reducing the number of bacteria present on the surface. Although some may consider disinfection to be optional, effective cleaning with hot water and soap is absolutely essential.

Remember to rinse off any soap or other chemicals used for cleaning or disinfection after use and be sure to follow the manufacturer's instructions on any cleaning product that is used.

HARMFUL BACTERIA

The main bugs of concern when curing meats are the ones that may be familiar to anyone who has received some basic training in food hygiene. The harmful bacteria include *Listeria monocytogenes*, *Salmonella* and Shiga toxin-producing *E. coli* such as *E. coli O157*.

Listeria is an organism associated with the soil and with wet environments. The curing process, involving salting and drying, reduces the water activity of the food, making it less hospitable to the organism. *Salmonella* and *E. coli* can contaminate meat when the animals are being slaughtered; they can be the result of faecal contamination. The curing process can reduce the risk associated with these organisms, but it is important to buy meat from a reputable source and for it to have been slaughtered and butchered under conditions maintaining a high standard of hygiene.

There are other bacteria which pose a hazard when curing meat. Non-proteolytic *Clostridium botulinum* is a particularly dangerous bacteria which is able to produce a heat-resistant toxin that can make people seriously ill. It is controlled by increasing acidity of a food so as to reduce the pH below 5.0, increasing the level of aqueous salt above 3.5%, or decreasing the water activity below 0.97.

Non-proteolytic *Clostridium botulinum* can grow at temperatures typically encountered in the fridge but it is a slow-growing organism. In the UK, packs of fresh meat are often limited to a ten-day shelf life to limit the growth of the bacteria. It will not grow at temperatures below 3°C/37.4°F.

Salt, water activity, and in some cases acidity, can limit the growth of *Clostridium* in cured meat. In the early parts of the curing process conditions may not yet be able to achieve this control and it is therefore very important to control the temperature while the meat is curing. The use of sodium nitrate as a curing salt can also contribute to safety. Follow instructions provided in each of the recipes very carefully.

PARASITIC WORMS

Parasitic worms are also of concern when curing meat and fish. In the UK, the National Health Service recommends freezing salmon if it is to be eaten raw. It should be frozen for at least 4 days at a maximum of −15°C/5°F in order to kill the *Anisakis* worm which can sometimes parasitise it.

Parasitic worms are known to affect many fish species including cod, mackerel, herring and monkfish. The UK Food Standards Agency advise that fish which is to be served raw should be frozen to an even lower temperature, of −20°C/−4°F, for 24 hours and that this temperature must be reached within the thickest part of the fish.

RIGHT Testing the pH of fermented salami mixture is important to ensure that process targets have been achieved and the food is safe

Trichinella is a parasitic worm associated with pigs. There is a mandatory testing program for *Trichinella* in domestic pigs in the EU which has reduced the incidence of infection. Similar eradication programs and rules prohibiting the feeding of raw meat to pigs has reduced the rate of infections in the USA.

The US Center for Disease Control and Prevention advises that curing, drying or smoking meat does not kill infective worms effectively. They recommend that pork which is less than 15cm/6in thick is frozen for at least 20 days at a temperature of −15°C/5°F, but advise that worms which infect wild game species may be more resistant to freezing. Several wild animals including rats are known to carry parasitic worms, and smallholders should ensure that their pigs are not exposed to rat carcasses.

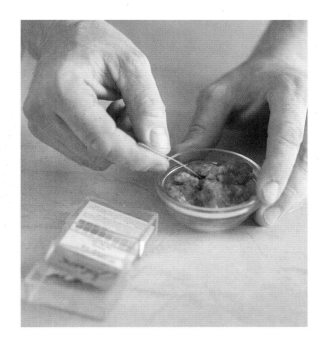

SALAMI &
AIR-DRIED CUTS

Instantly recognisable, this chapter features some familiar items on the charcuterie platter. Some, such as Bresaola, Lomo, Lardo and Coppa, are made from whole cuts of beef or pork which are salted and then slowly air-dried to remove moisture. As well as preserving them, the curing and drying process concentrates the flavour of the meat.

The salami recipes follow a similar process of salt-curing and air-drying, but here the meat is ground-up and flavoured. Fermentation with a starter culture helps to acidify the salami, which can impart a tangy flavour to it, but which also helps to preserve the meat. These recipes call for a little patience due to the long curing times and some require special equipment or ingredients, but all are well worth the effort.

AIR-DRIED HAM

Prosciutto di Parma, Jamón Serrano, Jamón Iberico, Jambon de Bayonne, Tyrolean Speck... some of the most famous charcuterie in the world all follow one basic technique – curing a pork leg in salt and then air-drying it to remove moisture.

While the size and cost of the pork leg can discourage some from undertaking this longer-term charcuterie project, there are few things as rewarding as cutting into a home-cured ham, and the economics cannot be questioned: sliced hams typically cost around three or four times as much as the meat used to make them.

Typically cured without added herbs or spices, the flavour of the meat is of prime importance and it is worth sourcing the best quality pork to ensure the best result.

The unique qualities of each type of ham can arise from subtle differences in curing conditions as well as the specific breed of pig, such as the famed black-footed Iberico pig of Spain. The flavour of the finished ham does not just rest on genetics though – the marbling of the muscle tissue with the fat, that is the key to flavour and mouthfeel in the ham, is also influenced by the diet and level of activity enjoyed by the animal.

The ham recipe is best started in the spring or autumn, when temperatures are cooler and when there are fewer flies buzzing around. It can be disappointing to discover that your ham is infested with maggots and the only option at that stage would be to discard the meat.

Fully cured hams are safe to store at ambient temperature and there is a rustic charm to the hams that are commonly seen hanging across Spain, from the tapas bars of Jerez to the Pintxos bars of San Sebastian. The temperature should be carefully controlled during salting and the early part of the curing process however, to prevent the growth of some particularly unpleasant bugs, and strict hygiene standards are required to minimise contamination.

Find a good-sized and well-proportioned leg of pork of about 7kg/15lb. A smaller leg could be used, which will cut down the curing time, but it will tend to become dry more quickly and there will be less usable meat left after trimming. Weigh the leg precisely before starting to cure it. You will need a large plastic or wooden box, big enough to fit the ham and also to be stored at the correct temperature.

SMOKING HAM

Some hams, such as Schwarzwälder Schinken from the Black Forest in Germany, are cold-smoked after salting but before the final stages of air-drying. Some moisture is lost during the smoking process, which takes place over several weeks, the outside of the ham taking on a blackened appearance. For more information, see pages 225–226.

INGREDIENTS

Pork leg (on the bone), weighing around 7kg/15lb

Curing Salt #2, 2.5g/¹⁄₁₆ oz per 1 kg/2.2lb of meat, optional (this must be measured accurately for the exact quantity of meat being used; see the notes on curing salts on pages 16–19 and always follow the manufacturer's instructions)

Pure dried vacuum (PDV) salt, approximately 10–20kg/22–44lb

White wine vinegar or cider vinegar (up to 100ml/3½fl oz, approximately)

Olive oil (up to 100ml/3½fl oz, approximately)

1 The leg can be washed prior to curing but do dry it well before salting. Trim off any loose scraps of meat, which will tend to become tough during curing. The femoral artery should also be drained of blood if there is any still present. To do this, squeeze along the inside of the leg, running up the bone from the foot to the ball of the hip joint. Weigh the leg carefully.

2 If curing salts are used, they must be weighed out very carefully and mixed well into the PDV salt to ensure even distribution. Curing salts are toxic if the dose is exceeded but they do inhibit the growth of harmful bacteria. If not used, an exceptionally high level of hygiene during butchery of the meat, and strict control of temperature during salting, are vital. Scatter a layer of PDV salt in the base of a plastic or wooden box just big enough to hold the leg.

3 Place in the leg and pour in the remaining salt mix, ensuring all the meat is completely covered.

4 The leg should be left in the salt for 2–3 days per 1 kg/2.2lb of meat. A weight can be placed on top of the salt if necessary; make sure that all parts of the leg remain covered with the salt during that time, ensure that it is protected from pests, and check the temperature each day. The temperature should be no more than 3°C/37°F during salting to prevent the growth of harmful bacteria. If the ambient temperature is too warm, then the leg should be moved to a refrigerator. When it is time to remove it from the salt, wash and dry the leg carefully before weighing it. Record the weight and keep this in a safe place as it will be essential to calculate weight loss during drying later.

5 The leg should be wrapped carefully but loosely in muslin, the corners of which should be gathered and knotted. This will help to keep dust and flies off.

6 Wrap some rope around the foot of the ham and hang it in a cool dry place – an airy larder or a meat safe. A humid environment will cause the ham to spoil. The temperature should be maintained at 12–18°C/53–64°F.

7 Weigh the ham periodically during drying and rub off any surface moulds using a little vinegar. The cleaned ham can be rubbed with olive oil before re-wrapping.

8 The ham should be ready to eat once it has lost at least one third of its original weight. In practice this may take several months as a minimum, but the ham can be hung for much longer to intensify the flavour if you prefer.

9 Once the ham is ready, the leg can be cleaned with vinegar and oiled again.

10 The ham should be stored at ambient temperature as this will result in the best flavour. Trimmed pieces of ham, however, should be covered and refrigerated to keep them in best condition.

CARVING THE HAM

Before cutting the ham, secure it in a ham-clamp with the thin back of the leg uppermost. This is the best part of the leg with a good amount of fat marbling the meat. The yellowish fat under the rind should be trimmed off prior to cutting as it will taste rancid. However as the rind protects the uncut parts of the ham, take care not to remove more than is necessary.

The ham is carved by hand, using a sharp, flexible carving knife. Slice thin layers from the top, keeping the cut face as flat as possible. The face can be protected with some clingfilm or food wrap after each carving, and the ham loosely covered with some muslin.

Once the bone is reached, free the meat from it using a thin boning knife, cutting parallel to the bone, and continue to slice the ham as before. The ham can be turned over and the front side of the leg sliced in the same way once the meat from the back has been enjoyed.

LOMO

This recipe for cured pork tenderloin brings with it the evocative flavours of Spain. Tenderloin is also called 'fillet' and is sometimes encountered in cross section in a loin chop where it is the disc of darker meat nestled beside the bone.

After being marinated in salt, garlic and smoked paprika for several days, the pork may be sliced and fried immediately or hung to dry over weeks and months. I describe both options below. Fried quickly for only a few minutes, this paprika- and garlic-infused pork tenderloin is probably my favourite way to cook pork. For those able to delay gratification for a little longer, the air-dried version of the lomo concentrates the flavours of the meat, which can become almost translucent when sliced. I tend to omit some of the salt if I know I am going straight to the cooked version.

The small diameter of the lomo means that the drying time can be much shorter than some of the hams and salamis covered elsewhere in this book, and it can be an inexpensive introduction to curing meat.

The flavours imparted into the meat by the pimenton are complex and smoky, with a lingering savoury finish. Whether it is cooked or dried, the distinctive and inviting flavour of lomo needs the subtlety of pimenton dulce (Spanish sweet smoked paprika) rather than the heat of the Hungarian variety of paprika.

Lomo makes an excellent addition to a charcuterie platter, contrasting wonderfully with the fennel-dominant flavours of the Italian-style salamis.

INGREDIENTS

Pork tenderloin, weighing approximately 450g/1lb

2 cloves garlic

30ml/2 tbsp olive oil

10ml/2 tsp pimenton (sweet smoked paprika)

18g/⅝oz pure dried vacuum (PDV) salt

5cm/2in fibrous casing

1 Peel and crush the cloves of garlic and add them to the olive oil with the smoked paprika.

2 Weigh and add the salt and mix the ingredients together well to form a thick paste. Weigh the tenderloin and record the weight – you will need this later to calculate the moisture loss.

3 Rub the paste over the tenderloin, making sure that the sides are evenly covered.

4 The tenderloin should be placed in a zip-lock or vacuum-pack plastic bag and kept in the refrigerator while the salt is adsorbed and the flavours infuse into the meat. The spice paste should be rubbed into the tenderloin each day to ensure that the meat is evenly coated, however this can be done quite easily through the bag. It is quite normal for the pork to release a small amount of water into the spice paste.

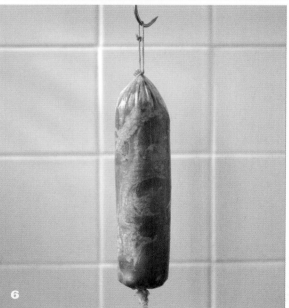

5 When the lomo has been cured for 7 days, rub off the excess spice paste and squeeze the cured tenderloin into a casing just big enough to fit it. It will take a little effort to get the tenderloin into the casing. Try to exclude as much air as possible while stuffing the casing and knotting the ends. It is possible to dry the lomo without the casing, but I have always preferred the results with it – the casing protects the outside of the meat as it dries and helps to prevent it from becoming mouldy. Weigh the lomo again just before hanging it and record the weight.

6 Hang the lomo in a meat safe or cool larder to allow it to dry. The temperature should be maintained at 5–8°C/41–47°F for the first month, then increased to 13–16°C/55–61°F for an additional 3–4 weeks. The meat can be rubbed with a little vinegar if any rogue moulds start to grow on it. The relative humidity should be around 75% during drying (see notes on page 28).

7 It should be ready to eat once it has lost 35–40% of its initial weight, as recorded at the start of curing, but it can be dried for longer according to preference. This is achieved once the meat reaches 0.65, but not less than 0.60, times its initial weight.

TO SERVE Score the dried casing with a sharp knife and peel it back to expose the meat below. As the casing helps to protect the meat below, only peel back as much as you need. Slice the lomo into thin discs approximately 2mm in thickness. The cut face can be protected by a strip of clingfilm. If the lomo is sliced again after several days, it is best to discard the top slice which may have started to become brown.

COOKED LOMO

1 Following the basic recipe on page 44, make up the marinating paste with crushed garlic, olive oil and smoked paprika, but also add a generous half teaspoon each of dried oregano and dried thyme. Use just half a teaspoon of salt. Mix the ingredients well, stirring in enough olive oil to make a thick paste.

2 Rub the paste over the tenderloin, making sure that the sides are evenly covered. The tenderloin should be placed in a zip-lock bag and this should be kept in the refrigerator while the salt is adsorbed and the flavours infuse into the meat. The spice paste should be rubbed again into the tenderloin each day to ensure that the meat is evenly coated. This can be done quite easily through the bag. It is normal for the pork to release a small amount of water into the spice paste as it cures.

3 When the meat has been cured for 2–3 days, it can be taken out and sliced into thin discs around 1cm/½in thick.

4 Heat a non-stick pan with a little oil until it is very hot and fry the discs of meat for a minute on each side until cooked through.

5 Serve them immediately with a squeeze of lemon juice and a scattering of finely chopped parsley. These make attractive and delicious tapas bites or canapes, served on little cocktail sticks.

LARDO

Unusual and intense, this salty, rich-flavoured cured pork fat can be cut like salami or coppa and makes a delightful addition to any charcuterie platter as well as being a great source of flavour in cooking.

The depth of flavour of many meats is associated with the fat. In the case of lardo, which is cured back fat carrying no lean meat, the taste is particularly intense, being infused as it cures with the flavours of black pepper, rosemary and garlic. The cure ingredients can vary by producer, and may be limited to these basic ingredients or might include a small quantity of oregano, sage, cinnamon or nutmeg.

Its most famous incarnation, Lardo di Colonnata, was granted a Protected Geographical Indication (PGI) by the European Union in 2004. The PGI is a protection granted to products with specific characteristics, unique to the area in which they are produced and, like a trademark, protects the name from being used by products which do not meet the quality standards required or are not manufactured in the correct geographical area. Lardo di Colonnata is named after a town in Tuscany in the north of Italy. The area is renowned for its marble quarries, and the lardo made in the region is famous for being cured in a marble curing basin, called a conche, which is known to have been used since at least the 17th century. The conche provides a cool, dark place in which the lardo can be cured, away from the light that can cause the fat to become oxidised and taste rancid. In Colonnata, the pork backs are cured within 72 hours of slaughter, the freshness of the meat

ensuring that oxidative rancidity is prevented as much as possible. In some, usually leaner, charcuterie products such as the Spanish air-dried hams, this rancidity can contribute in a small way to the flavour profile. Excessive breakdown of the fat, however, can produce significant flavour defects, and I advise using very fresh fat in the preparation of lardo.

The production of Lardo di Colonnata is seasonal and is now restricted to the months of September to May, although historically the pigs would have been slaughtered and the pork cured in the coldest months of the year, January and February, when the ambient temperatures would have helped to control the growth of some of the less desirable spoilage bacteria and pathogens. For your own lardo, careful temperature control during the curing process will be necessary to ensure safety, and the early part of the curing process should take place in the refrigerator. Read the notes on cleaning, disinfection and food safety on pages 34–35 for advice on the use of pork in the preparation of ready-to-eat foods.

You can serve slices of lardo with crusty bread as part of a charcuterie platter. The thin slice of rind can be left on for presentation purposes though it can be a bit too tough and chewy for many people. Remove the rind if making canapes or if using the lardo in cooking. Chopped lardo can be fried and used to replace pancetta in pasta dishes such as tagliatelle carbonara, or stirred though borlotti beans cooked in a reduced passata sauce along with a splash of wine vinegar, garlic and oregano.

INGREDIENTS

One slab of pork back fat, skin on, weighing around 1–1.5kg/2lb 2oz–3lb 3oz, as thick as possible

200g/7oz pure dried vacuum (PDV) salt

Curing Salt #2, 2.5g/¹⁄₁₆ oz per 1 kg/2.2lb of meat, optional (this must be measured accurately for the exact quantity of meat being used; see the notes on curing salts on pages 16–19 and always follow the manufacturer's instructions)

14g/½oz sugar

5–6 cloves garlic

1 bunch rosemary

2–3 bay leaves

5ml/1 tsp crushed black pepper

2.5ml/½ tsp ground cinnamon or nutmeg

2.5ml/½ tsp oregano or sage, optional

1 Rinse the back fat and pat it dry with kitchen paper. To prepare the cure, weigh out the salts and sugar, adjusting the quantities for the exact weight of the back fat.

2 Peel and roughly chop the garlic. Wash and chop the rosemary into approximately 2cm/¾in lengths, and tear the bay leaves in half. Add the garlic, rosemary, black pepper, cinnamon or nutmeg, bay leaves and oregano or sage, if using, to the salt and sugar. Mix all the cure ingredients together well. In the absence of a marble basin, place the fat into a non-reactive bowl, plastic tub or (easiest) zip-lock or vacuum-pack bag. Pour in the cure and make sure that the fat is evenly coated on all sides. Tie the bag or cover the container.

3 The back fat should be kept in the refrigerator at a temperature of 3–5°C/37–41°F and left to cure for at least 10–14 days per kg (5–6 days per lb). It should be covered, to keep it in the dark. Check it every 2–3 days and make sure that the cure is evenly spread across the back fat, redistributing it if necessary. If using a plastic bag, the cure can be rubbed in through the bag as it is less messy.

4 At the end of the curing time, remove the lardo and wash off any excess cure before patting it dry with a paper towel. It may have shrunk slightly and will feel firmer to the touch.

5 The lardo should be hung on a butcher's hook or bacon comb in a cool, dark place for at least 14 days. It will be ready to eat at the end of that time and will feel very firm.

TO SERVE When you are ready to serve it, slice the lardo very finely using a sharp knife or a meat slicer. As with pancetta, to improve the keeping qualities, only slice as much as you need each time and cover the cut face of the lardo with some clingfilm or food wrap to stop it from drying out. Any surface moulds which appear on the rind should be scrubbed off with a little vinegar as they appear. Wrap the lardo in greaseproof or waxed paper to stop it drying out excessively and keep it in the refrigerator or a cool larder until needed. Once it is ready, it is best enjoyed within a few weeks.

COPPA

Coppa is an incredible cured pork product with a status approaching that of legend amongst those in the know. Coppa looks like a salami, marbled with delicious fat, but it is in fact a whole cut of meat – taken from a single muscle which runs along the top of the shoulder.

Alternatively known as 'capocollo', which translates as 'head (of the) neck', the cut of meat used to make coppa is sometimes sold as a collar or neck fillet. This is also often encountered as part of the joint that is sometimes referred to as a 'pork butt' or 'Boston butt' – a cut from the very top of the shoulder, incorporating the wonderfully marbled collar meat which is commonly used to prepare pulled pork dishes. Cutting the muscle from a larger pork butt should yield a coppa of at least 1kg/2lb 2oz, and also leaves a good quantity of spare shoulder meat which can be incorporated into the meat mixture for your salami, or seasoned and flavoured with fennel then roasted slowly as a treat for the busy home charcutier.

Coppa is an easy meat to cure, requiring none of the mincing and stuffing equipment required to make traditional salami. The small amount of effort to prepare coppa is more than repaid, following a few months' curing and drying time. As with other cured meats prepared from primal cuts or whole muscles, there is no starter culture added during preparation. Safety in this case depends on accurately weighing the salt and curing salts, good hygiene during preparation, and adequate temperature control throughout the process rather than the presence of a competitive microflora. Follow the recipe carefully, paying attention to the temperatures specified, and calculating the salt and curing salt exactly, based upon the weight of meat.

There are several examples of traditional products made across Italy which have been awarded Protected Designation of Origin (PDO) or Protected Geographical Indication (PGI) status, such as Coppa Piacentina or Coppa di Parma. These products are manufactured in the region of Emilia Romagna in the north of Italy, an area renowned for the quality of its traditional charcuterie and cheesemaking. The ambient temperature in the region averages 10–15°C/50–59°F across the year, falling below 8°C/46°F during the colder autumn and winter months. Pigs were traditionally slaughtered during these months, typically in November or December. While some people may hold traditional forms of food production as being generally uncontrolled processes, often citing them as a reason not to worry about careful temperature control, it is nonetheless easy to see how the geography and weather conditions within particular regions can form an intrinsic part of the natural food safety of the products made there.

It is possible to cure pork loin in the same way as the neck or collar, the resulting product often being referred to as 'lonzino'. And after succeeding with coppa you might like to try making bresaola, using lean topside of beef (see page 60).

INGREDIENTS

Neck end or 'Boston butt', cut from the top of a pork shoulder which should yield a 1–1.5kg/2lb 2oz –3lb 3oz coppa muscle (see method below)

Curing Salt #2, 2.5g/¹⁄₁₆ oz per 1 kg/2.2lb of meat, optional (this must be measured accurately for the exact quantity of meat being used; see the notes on curing salts on pages 16–19 and always follow the manufacturer's instructions)

40g/1½oz pure dried vacuum (PDV) salt

5ml/1 tsp ground white pepper

2.5ml/½ tsp cinnamon

5ml/1 tsp juniper berries, crushed

1.5ml/¼ tsp garlic powder

Large fibrous or natural salami casing

a pinch of *Penicillium nalgiovense* mould culture (about 0.4g), optional

MOULDS ON SALAMI

First identified in a salami factory in Italy, *Penicillium nalgiovense* has a long history of use on salami but it is not the only species of mould associated with these foods. In 2015, scientists reported the identification of a novel species of *Penicillium* in the International Journal of Food Microbiology. They named it *Penicillium salami.*

1 Place the meat skin side down on a chopping board. If the spine is present, use a boning knife to remove the bones. Locate the shoulder blade; the coppa muscle can be found at the narrow end, on the opposite side.

2 Turn over the meat, slice off the skin and follow the seam of fat to free the coppa from the rest of the shoulder. Avoid damaging the coppa by cutting too deeply into it.

3 Remove and weigh the coppa and record the weight as it will be needed to calculate the moisture loss during drying.

4 Measure out the curing salt on an accurate set of scales and mix it well with the PDV salt. Add the ground white pepper, cinnamon, crushed juniper berries and garlic powder. Place the coppa muscle in a zip-lock or vacuum-pack plastic bag. Pour in the salt and spice curing mixture, and rub over, ensuring that the meat is as evenly coated as possible. Seal the bag and place it in the refrigerator at 3–5°C/37–41°F for 14 days, turning the pork in the bag every other day to redistribute the cure around the meat.

5 Remove the coppa from the bag and rinse off any excess cure. Pat dry with a paper towel.

6 The coppa should be packed into a fibrous or large natural casing that is just big enough to hold it. Soak the casing for at least half an hour ahead of stuffing to make it easier. Rub the outside of the meat with a little olive oil if you have any difficulty getting it into the casing.

7 Work slowly and try to squeeze out all the air, forcing the coppa down into the casing. Tie the end with butcher's string to enclose the coppa, and trim off excess casing.

8 A butcher's net is then tied around the outside to maintain its shape while hanging.

9 Dissolve some *Penicillium nalgiovense* mould culture in a little water and rub it on the surface of the coppa. This will help to prevent growth of less desirable moulds during drying.

10 Hang the coppa in a meat safe or in a cool larder to allow it to dry. The temperature should be maintained at 10–12°C/50–54°F with humidity around 80%. This can be reduced to 75% as the coppa dries, but starting with too low a humidity will cause the casing to become hard and dry, preventing moisture loss from the core. It should be ready to eat once it has lost 30–35% of its initial weight, as recorded at the start of curing, but it can be dried for longer according to preference. Expect to hang the coppa for 2–3 months, depending on the size of the cut of meat used.

TO SERVE Cut off the netting and score the casing with a sharp knife. Peel it back as far as you intend to slice. Slice the coppa very finely either with a sharp carving knife or, better still, using a meat slicer. To store, the cut face can be protected by a small strip of clingfilm or food wrap.

The beautiful natural marbling of fat gives this cured meat a striking and distinctive appearance on the charcuterie platter.

BRESAOLA

An Italian classic, the translucent ruby colour of thinly-cut bresaola with its minimal marbling of fat hints at the intense meaty flavour of the beef that follows. This recipe truly is a celebration of beef; be sure to source the best quality meat that you can find.

One of the most highly regarded traditional cured meats of Italy, the Bresaola della Valtellina was awarded a Protected Geographical Indication (PGI) in 1996. This bresaola is made in a valley in Lombardy, in the extreme north of Italy and not far from the Swiss border, a region well known for the production of cow's milk cheeses including bitto, a seasonally-made hard cheese which can be aged for many years. There are records of both cheese and cured meats from this area for over 500 years and it is perhaps not surprising that an area renowned for its dairy production should also develop recipes for cured products made from beef.

The recipe is much more widespread these days, with examples of artisanal bresaola being made all over the world. It is a fairly easy recipe to follow, requiring little in the way of specialist equipment. Like coppa, lomo and pancetta, this is made from a larger slab of meat that, unlike salami, is not minced during its production.

The cut of beef which should be used to prepare bresaola is from the top of the hindquarter of the animal. Silverside and topside work very well. In some places, such as the United States, these may form part of a larger cut referred to as the 'round' steak. This is a reasonably lean cut of beef, typically with a good amount of flavour. Because the beef cuts are so lean, they often have a slightly drier mouthfeel than the cured pork products. A very thin strip of meat will tend to become very dry and chewy so choose a good-sized, thick joint that will retain some tenderness during curing and drying. Trim off any excess fat from around the edges; it is less likely to develop rancidity than pork fat but it is harder and it is unlikely to enhance the mouthfeel of the bresaola.

INGREDIENTS

Beef topside, silverside or round, 1.5kg/3lb 3oz

50ml/2fl oz red wine

Curing Salt #2, 2.5g/¹⁄₁₆oz per 1 kg/2.2lb of meat, optional (this must be measured accurately for the exact quantity of meat being used; see the notes on curing salts on pages 16–19 and always follow the manufacturer's instructions)

40g/1½oz pure dried vacuum (PDV) salt

2.5ml/½ tsp ground black pepper

1.5ml/¼ tsp chopped fresh rosemary

1.5ml/¼ tsp dried thyme or oregano

1.5ml/¼ tsp dried juniper berries, crushed

2.5ml/½ tsp ground nutmeg

Large fibrous or natural salami casing

1 Using a sharp knife, trim any scraps of meat from the outside of the beef as these can become quite tough during curing. Also remove any outer layers of fat. Weigh the trimmed joint of beef and record the weight. You will need this to calculate the quantity of curing salts but also the moisture loss during drying.

2 Place the beef into a plastic zip-lock or vacuum-pack bag and pour in the red wine. Leave it in the refrigerator at 3–5°C/37–41°F overnight. The following day, open the bag and discard the wine.

3 Measure out the curing salt accurately for the exact quantity of meat being used and mix it with the PDV salt. Add the pepper, rosemary, thyme or oregano, juniper berries and nutmeg. Pour the cure ingredients into the bag, coating the meat as evenly as possible.

4 Seal the bag and place it in the refrigerator at 3–5°C/37–41°F for 14 days, turning the beef in the bag every other day to redistribute the cure. After 2 weeks, remove the meat from the bag. It should look darker and will feel firmer. Rinse off the excess cure, and pat dry with kitchen paper.

5 The beef is then packed into a fibrous or large natural casing that is just big enough to hold it and which has been soaked for at least half an hour ahead of stuffing. If it is difficult to fill the casing, rub the outside of the meat with a little olive oil. Working slowly, carefully ease the beef in, squeezing all the air out of the casing. Tie the end with butcher's string. A butcher's net can be tied around the outside, principally to help to maintain its shape as it dries but it also adds to the visual appeal of the hanging meat.

6 Hang the bresaola to dry in a meat safe or in a cool larder until it loses 35–40% of its weight. This may take several months depending on the size of the cut of beef. The temperature should be maintained steadily at 10–12°C/50–54°F with humidity around 80%. Too low a humidity in the early stages will cause the outside of the meat to harden, preventing the core from drying properly.

TO SERVE Cut off the netting and score the casing with a sharp knife, peeling it back as far as you intend to slice. Slice very finely either with a carving knife or a meat slicer. The cut face should be protected with a strip of clingfilm or food wrap to prevent it from drying out. If several days pass since the bresaola was last carved, discard the first slice which is likely to have dried out. Wrap the remaining bresaola in greaseproof paper to prevent it from drying out and to protect the surface from contamination.

SPICE MIXTURES

The spice mixture can also be enhanced with ¼ teaspoon of star anise seeds which, while not traditional, marries beautifully with the flavour of beef. Do not be afraid to experiment with your own unique spice mixture, but keep a note of it; discovering the perfect blend can lead to frustration if you cannot later recall the spices used.

SALAMI

Few things can be as delightfully rustic-looking as various shapes and sizes of salami hanging above the delicatessen counter. The flavour and texture of the different varieties depend on the herbs and spices used, and the distribution of fat, but the process is remarkably similar for each.

Salami production follows the same kind of processes as sausage-making, and is salted and dried like other cured meats such as coppa or lomo. It is however unusual in that it also relies on fermentation to help prevent the growth of harmful bacteria. This is important as, unlike the other cured meats, it is made of minced meat rather than a whole cut. Many of the harmful bacteria that we might associate with cured meat is found on the outside, which begins to dry earlier than the inside. By mincing the meat, we risk spreading any contaminants into the centre, and the additional 'hurdles' introduced by the fermentation starter mitigate this to some degree.

The fermentation which takes place here relies on lactic acid bacteria similar to those used in cheesemaking, rather than *Lactococcus*. The most commonly encountered species are *Pediococcus*, *Lactobacillus* or Coagulase-negative Staphylococci such as *Staphylococcus xylosus*. These are fairly hardy organisms sometimes associated with other traditional fermented foods such as sauerkraut. Coagulase-positive Staphylococci are often associated with the flavour development and rind pigmentation of the sticky, orange or pink washed rind cheeses.

As a general rule the acidification should take place over several days and should be carried out at a constant temperature. The acidification will fail if the temperature is too low during fermentation, which will compromise the safety of the salami. Similarly, acidification which is too rapid may not allow the growth of nitrate-reducing bacteria in the starter, which are needed to contribute to 'fixing' the pink colour of the salami. (See pages 16–19 for more detail on curing salts, which can contribute to salami pigmentation.)

The Canadian Food Inspection Agency has comprehensive manufacturing guidelines available on their website. Some of the information provided is more complex than is possible to interpret for the home charcutier, but their concept of 'degree-hours' is a useful guide to safe fermentation time, calculating the acidification period required to control the growth of *Staphylococcus aureus*, a pathogenic species of bacteria that can produce toxins which cause food poisoning. The recommended fermentation temperatures provided in the table on page 67 have been calculated with this guidance in mind.

For recipes which include beef, such as the Milano recipe, the fermentation time is longer and at a higher temperature, and the pH target is lower to

OPPOSITE Despite the similarity in the basic techniques employed, a wide variety of different salami products can be created, each to their own unique specification

control the risk of Shiga toxin-producing *E. coli* such as O157:H7. This bug is associated with cross-contamination of meat arising from faecal matter from infected animals and it has been identified in several studies. The risk can be minimised by scrupulous hygiene from the slaughterhouse onwards. The fermentation conditions required – typically 32°C/90°F for 7 days, sufficient to reach a pH of less than 4.6 – can be tricky for the amateur charcutier to maintain at home. Given this technical difficulty in meeting the recommendation at home, an alternative is to consider a 'sear and shave' approach.

The white mould which grows on the surface of the dried salami is typically *Penicillium nalgiovense*. This can be added deliberately as a culture or else its growth can be encouraged by hanging finished salamis alongside the newly made ones. There is a distinct benefit in adding these moulds especially to your first batches of salami. Their rapid growth can help to out-compete less desirable moulds which could cause the meat to spoil or may produce mycotoxins. Rogue moulds can also be inhibited by occasionally rubbing the salami with a little vinegar but, as moulds tend to be tolerant of low pH and low moisture, you may still need to remain vigilant for signs of growth during drying.

If all of this sounds a little scary, following a few simple instructions will minimise the risks posed by the less desirable organisms, and cutting into a home-made salami is an immensely satisfying reward for a morning's careful work.

Essential to achieving good texture in the finished salami, the correct mix of fat to lean meat is important. The cut, size and distribution of the fat plays a role in the character of the different types of salami. Fat helps to soften the mouthfeel, which will be firmer and drier when the fat is present as large, widely dispersed chunks, as in the Toscano-style, but softer when finely ground as in the Milano-style.

SEAR AND SHAVE

The UK Food Standards Agency recommends 'sear and shave' as a treatment to reduce the risk of *E. coli* O157 in burgers which are to be served less than fully cooked. Where the bacteria are present, they are located around the outside of the cut of meat. When a steak is served pink, the bacteria on the surface are inactivated by the heat, however mincing the steak distributes the contamination throughout the meat. Bacteria in the centre of a burger that is served rare may survive the cooking process.

However, if the meat is first seared to kill off the bacteria on the surface and then the outer layer of cooked meat is 'shaved' or chopped off, the pink meat below should be free from contamination by *E. coli* O157. This approach may also deal with the risk of contamination when preparing beef for charcuterie products that are served without cooking.

Searing and shaving should be carried out before the meat is chopped and minced. A thick, narrow block of meat is more suitable than a thin, wide slice. Sear the meat quickly in a hot pan for around 30 seconds to achieve a temperature of at least 65°C/149°F on each surface. Do not pierce the meat with a temperature probe while searing it. Remove it from the pan and slice off the outer layer of cooked meat. The pink meat underneath should now be free from contamination. (The shavings can be returned to the pan and fried up as a treat.)

TEMPERATURE °C	°F	FERMENTATION TIME	FERMENTATION SPEED
20	68.0	6 days	Slow
22	71.6	4 days	Medium
24*	75.2	3 days	Medium
26*	78.8	2½ days	Medium-Fast

*recommended temperatures

MILANO-STYLE SALAMI

Milano salami is made with pork shoulder and fat, which may be mixed with beef or veal; it is cut small to give a very even distribution of fat to lean meat.

INGREDIENTS

Pork shoulder, weighing 900g/2lb

Veal (or beef) fillet, rump or shoulder, 500g/1lb 2oz

Pork backfat, weighing 500g/1lb 2oz

0.5g Bactoferm T-SPX salami starter culture (or similar slow-acidifying culture used according to manufacturer's instructions)

Curing Salt #2, 2.5g/¹⁄₁₆oz per 1 kg/2.2lb of meat, optional (this must be measured accurately for the exact quantity of meat being used; see the notes on curing salts on pages 16–19 and always follow the manufacturer's instructions)

40g/1½oz pure dried vacuum (PDV) salt

3.5g/⅛oz sugar

5ml/1 tsp ground white pepper

2.5ml/½ tsp garlic powder or 2–4 cloves garlic, crushed

30ml/2 tbsp red wine

Fibrous casing and optional butcher's net

a pinch of *Penicillium nalgiovense* mould culture (about 0.4g), optional

1 Soak the fibrous salami casing in water for half an hour before filling it. Weigh the pork shoulder, veal or beef, and pork backfat, and chop them into evenly-sized chunks small enough to fit into the mincer. Before chopping the pork and veal, the surface of the meat can be seared and shaved as described on page 67, for additional food safety. If you like, you can place the chopped meat and fat in the freezer for 5–10 minutes before mincing it, to help make it firmer and easier to handle.

2 Grind all the chopped meat and fat through a 3–5mm/⅛–¼in mincer plate, into a small bowl. Mince a little of each of the ingredients in turn as this will make it easier to combine and ensure that the fat is evenly distributed.

3 Dissolve the starter culture into a tablespoon of water. Sprinkle it over the meat. Weigh the curing salt carefully, add it to the PDV salt and mix together very well. Add the salt mixture to the meat along with the sugar, white pepper, and garlic or garlic powder.

4 Add the red wine. Do not use wine which is old, oxidised (browning) or cork-tainted as the off-tastes will come through in the finished salami and ruin the flavour. Only use wine that you are happy to put in your glass and do not be overgenerous with it as that can cause the moisture level of this salami to rise too high, which can compromise safety.

5 Mix it all together very well. No matter how good the ingredients used, inadequate mixing at this stage will ruin the salami – at best, a quality issue but, at worst, a food safety issue due to inadequate salt distribution

6 Before casing, you can reserve a tablespoon of the mixture, rolled into a small patty, as a sample to monitor the pH development during fermentation. This can be done by chopping the sample up until it becomes a soft paste and checking with a pH meter or pH paper. The safety sample will need to be kept warm alongside the salami.

7 Pack the well-mixed salami ingredients into a sausage stuffer or use the filling nozzle on your mincer to fill the casings.

8 Place the casing over the end of the nozzle, making sure that the tip reaches the tied end of the casing. Crank the handle to begin filling, working slowly but steadily to avoid incorporating too much air into the casing.

9 Squeeze the meat down to the end of the casing. Push out the air and tie the end tightly with a length of butcher's string, securing it with a double knot. Weigh the salami and record the weight. You will need it to calculate weight loss during drying.

10 If liked, a butcher's net can be tied around the outside, to help to maintain its shape as it dries.

11 If using, dissolve the *Penicillium nalgiovense* in a few tablespoons of clean water and use a very clean or

gloved hand to rub it over the surface of the salami. If you are not using this mould culture then consider hanging your freshly-made salami alongside older examples which already have a good distribution of white mould on the surface.

12 Hang the salami in a warm, slightly humid room (preferably 24–26°C/75.2–78.8°F) for 2½ to 3 days. Monitor the temperature and pH by testing the sample throughout the hanging process – the temperature should be kept relatively stable and when checked, the pH should reach 5.30 or less by the end of the fermentation stage.

13 Once the fermentation is complete, hang the salami to dry at 12–15°C/53.6–59.0°F until it loses around 30% of its initial weight. This may take a couple of months depending on the diameter of casing used and the relative humidity during drying – which should be maintained around 85% at first. If conditions are too dry, however, the casing may harden which can trap moisture at the core of the salami causing it to spoil. The humidity should not be too high either; at over 90% the salami will be likely to develop patches of unsightly rogue moulds. After a period of several weeks drying, the humidity can be reduced slightly to around 70–75%. Once the salami has lost 30% of its initial weight, it can be served.

TO SERVE Remove the net, peel back the fibrous casing as far as you intend to slice the salami and cut it with a very sharp knife or an electric meat slicer. The cut face can be covered with clingfilm or food wrap to stop it drying.

FELINO-STYLE SALAMI

Felino is a mild-flavoured traditional salami originating from a town in the province of Parma, Italy. The product was awarded a Protected Geographical Indication (PGI) in 2013. The PGI specification sets clear rules on the origin of the pork, the cuts of meat used and the expected composition of the salami. The salami is made from belly and shoulder cuts which are usually taken from Landrace, Large White or Duroc pigs.

INGREDIENTS

Pork shoulder, weighing 600g/1lb 5oz

Belly pork with a generous amount of fat, weighing 400g/14oz

0.5g Bactoferm T-SPX salami starter culture (or similar slow-acidifying culture used according to manufacturer's instructions)

Curing Salt #2, 2.5g/¹⁄₁₆oz per 1 kg/2.2lb of meat, optional (this must be measured accurately for the exact quantity of meat being used; see the notes on curing salts on pages 16–19 and always follow the manufacturer's instructions)

21g/¾oz pure dried vacuum (PDV) salt

1.8g/¹⁄₁₆oz sugar

2.5ml/½ tsp coarsely ground black pepper

2 cloves garlic, crushed

30ml/2 tbsp dry white wine

5cm/2in fibrous casing

a pinch of *Penicillium nalgiovense* mould culture (about 0.4g)

1 Soak the fibrous salami casing in water at least half an hour before you intend to fill it. Weigh the pork shoulder and belly meat and chop into evenly-sized chunks. These should be small enough to fit into the mincer.

2 Mince the pork through an 8mm/⅜in mincer plate into a small bowl. Mince a little of each of the ingredients in turn as this will make it easier to mix and to ensure that the fat is evenly distributed. Some of the fat can be chopped rather than minced if you want some slightly larger chunks distributed through the salami.

3 Dissolve the starter culture into a tablespoon of water and sprinkle it over the meat. Weigh the curing salt very carefully, add it to the PDV salt and make sure that it is thoroughly mixed. Add the salt mixture, sugar, black pepper and crushed garlic to the meat, mixing it in well. It is essential that the salt is evenly distributed in the salami. Finally, mix in the dry white wine.

4 Pack the well-mixed salami ingredients into a sausage stuffer. Roll the casing over the end of the nozzle. Slowly cranking the handle, begin to fill the casing, making sure that as much air as possible is

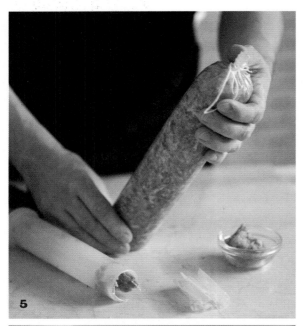

5

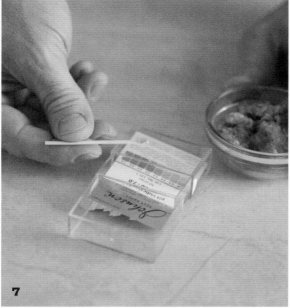

7

excluded. Remember to reserve a tablespoon of the mixture and roll it into a small patty. This should be kept warm alongside the salami and used as a sample to monitor pH development during fermentation.

5 Squeeze the air out of the end of the casing and tie the end twice with a length of butcher's string. Weigh the salami and record the weight carefully as you will need it to calculate moisture loss during drying.

6 Dissolve the *Penicillium nalgiovense* in a few tablespoons of clean water, and rub it gently on the surface of the salami using a very clean or gloved hand.

7 The salami should be left in a warm room at 24°C/75.2°F for 3 days as specified in the table on page 67. Monitor the temperature by testing the sample throughout; a steady temperature should be maintained during fermentation and the pH should come down to 5.30 by the end of this time.

8 Once the fermentation is complete, hang the salami at 12–15°C/53.6–59.0°F. Humidity should be 80–90% and the air should be circulating slightly rather than still. Drying will take several weeks, depending on the size of salami and ambient humidity. The salami is ready to eat once it has lost 30% of its initial weight.

TO SERVE When slicing, the casing should be peeled off just as far as you intend to cut. Slice the salami finely using a sharp knife or an electric slicer. The cut face can be covered with clingfilm or food wrap to stop it drying.

TOSCANO-STYLE SALAMI

A dry-textured, meaty salami with large grains of fat widely dispersed throughout the sausage, this makes an interesting counterpoint to the softer-textured Milano-style.

Pork shoulder, weighing 750g/1lb 10oz

Pork backfat, weighing 300g/10½oz

0.5g Bactoferm T-SPX salami starter culture (or similar slow-acidifying culture used according to manufacturer's instructions)

Curing Salt #2, 2.5g/¹⁄₁₆oz per 1 kg/2.2lb of meat, optional (this must be measured accurately for the exact quantity of meat being used; see the notes on curing salts on pages 16–19 and always follow the manufacturer's instructions)

27g/1oz pure dried vacuum (PDV) salt

1.8g/¹⁄₁₆oz sugar

2.5ml/½ tsp ground white pepper

2.5ml/½ tsp fennel seeds

2 cloves garlic, crushed

30ml/2 tbsp dry white wine

5cm/2in fibrous casing

a pinch of *Penicillium nalgiovense* mould culture (about 0.4g)

1 First, put the salami casing in water to soak for at least half an hour before it is to be filled. Then, weigh out the pork shoulder and chop it into chunks that are small enough to fit into the mincer.

2 The pork backfat is not minced for the Toscano-style salami but, instead, should be chopped into cubes. These may be slightly uneven but should be roughly 1cm/½in cubes.

3 Mince the pork through an 8mm/⅜in plate into a small bowl. Dissolve the starter culture into a tablespoon of water and sprinkle it over the meat. Add in the chopped backfat.

4 Weigh the curing salt accurately on a set of scales. Add it to the PDV salt and make sure that it is thoroughly mixed.

5 Add the salt mixture, sugar, white pepper, fennel, crushed garlic and wine to the meat and mix it in well to ensure that the salt is evenly distributed.

6 Pack the salami ingredients into a sausage stuffer. Roll the casing over the end of the nozzle. Begin cranking the handle, supporting the case as it is filled. Exclude as much air as possible when filling the casings. A sample tablespoon 'patty' of the mixture should be reserved at this stage, to be used to monitor the pH development of the salami during fermentation.

7 Squeeze the air out of the end of the casing, and tie the end twice with a length of butcher's string before weighing the salami. This weight should be recorded as it will be needed to calculate moisture loss during drying.

8 The *Penicillium nalgiovense* mould culture should now be dissolved in a few tablespoons of clean water, and rubbed gently on the outside of the casing using a very clean or gloved hand.

9 Leave the salami in a warm room at 24°C/75.2°F for three days as specified in the table on page 67. Monitor the temperature regularly by testing the sample (kept alongside the salami for the duration). A steady temperature should be maintained during fermentation and the pH should come down to 5.30 by the end of this time.

10 After the fermentation stage, hang the salami to dry at 12–15°C/53.6–59°F. The humidity in the drying room should be maintained at 80–90% with gentle air movement. The salami will be left for several weeks, until it loses around 30% of its initial weight.

TO SERVE Once ready, the casing should be peeled off as far as you intend to cut. The salami should be sliced finely using an electric meat slicer; as the salami is often firmer and drier than the other types described here, it can be harder to cut using a knife. The cut face can be covered with clingfilm or food wrap to stop it drying.

SALAMI FINNOCHIONA

Finnochiona is a famous fennel-rich salami, made in Tuscany where there is an abundance of wild fennel. Our recipe takes its influence from this salami, giving a pleasant, fresh-tasting cured meat with a good distribution of finely-cut fat.

INGREDIENTS

Pork shoulder, weighing 600g/1lb 3oz

Pork backfat, weighing 400g/14oz

0.5g Bactoferm T-SPX salami starter culture (or similar slow- acidifying culture according to manufacturer's instructions)

Curing Salt #2, 2.5g/¹⁄₁₆oz per 1 kg/2.2lb of meat, optional (this must be measured accurately for the exact quantity of meat being used; see the notes on curing salts on pages 16–19 and always follow the manufacturer's instructions)

21g/¾oz pure dried vacuum (PDV) salt

1.8g/¹⁄₁₆oz sugar

5ml/1 tsp fennel seeds

2.5ml/½tsp coarsely ground black pepper

2 cloves garlic, crushed

30ml/2 tbsp dry white wine

5cm/2in fibrous casing

a pinch of *Penicillium nalgiovense* mould culture

1 Soak the fibrous salami casing in water for half an hour before filling it. Weigh out the pork shoulder and backfat, before chopping them into evenly-sized chunks small enough to fit into the mincer. If you like, you can place the chopped meat and fat in the freezer for 5–10 minutes before mincing it, to help make it firmer and easier to handle.

2 Mince the pork shoulder and backfat through an 8mm/⅜in plate. Alternate between the fat and lean meat when mincing as it will make them easier to combine.

3 Dissolve the starter culture into a tablespoon of water and sprinkle it over the meat.

4 If using curing salt, weigh it out very carefully. Add it to the PDV salt and make sure that it is thoroughly mixed. Add the salt mixture, sugar, fennel, black pepper and crushed garlic to the meat, and add the dry white wine.

5 Mix everything in very well, as it is essential that all the salt is evenly distributed.

6 After mixing, pack the salami ingredients into a sausage stuffer. A tablespoon of the mixture can be reserved as a sample and kept alongside the salami to be used to monitor pH development during the fermentation.

7

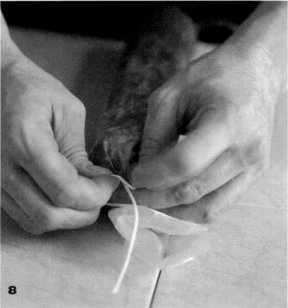

8

7 Roll the casing over the end of the nozzle and begin to fill it, excluding as much air as possible.

8 Tie the end of the casing twice with a length of butcher's string to seal the salami. It is important to exclude as much air as possible or it could allow the tip of the salami to become mouldy.

9 Dissolve the *Penicillium nalgiovense* in a few tablespoons of clean water and rub it gently on the surface of the salami using a very clean or gloved hand. Record the weight of the salami so that moisture loss during drying can be calculated.

10 The salami should be dried at 24°C/75.2°F for 3 days (see table on page 67). Avoid fluctuations in temperature where possible. Humidity should be maintained at 80–90% with gentle air circulation. Monitor the temperature regularly by testing the sample. A steady temperature should be maintained during fermentation and the pH should come down to 5.30 by the end of this time.

11 Once the fermentation is complete, hang the salami at 12–15°C/53.6–59°F. It should be dried until it loses around 30% of its initial weight and this may take several weeks. Using some vinegar, rub off any unwanted rogue moulds, other than the white *Penicillium nalgiovense*, that form on the rind.

TO SERVE Once dried and ready to eat, the casing should be peeled off as far as required to slice. Slice the salami as finely as possible using a sharp knife or meat slicer. The cut face can be covered with clingfilm or food wrap to stop it drying.

SALAMI PICCANTE

Not for the faint-hearted, this small salami has tangy, sour and spicy chilli flavours and makes an excellent addition to a charcuterie platter for those who like their cured meats with a bit of a kick. It is good served as an antipasto alongside olives, artichoke hearts or some crusty bread. It pairs well with crisp white wine though some light reds and rose wines can also work well.

Unlike previous salamis in the chapter, this recipe uses fast fermentation to acidify the meat and outgrow harmful bacteria. The speed of fermentation means that the salami can be enjoyed much sooner than the slower-fermenting varieties. The recipe therefore calls for a fast-acting starter culture and careful control of the temperature of fermentation to achieve a low pH in a short period of time. Make sure the starter culture can ferment either the dextrose or ordinary sugar (sucrose) you intend to use. Your starter supplier should be able to provide a product specification sheet which gives this information.

The meat for this salami should be of good quality, sourced from a reputable supplier, and held under refrigerated conditions throughout its storage. The fast fermentation process alone cannot guarantee safety if the meat has been produced unhygienically or following temperature abuse. Follow the simple instructions and advice in the food safety section on pages 34–35.

Fermentation in salami production and cheesemaking has been used historically as a way of preserving foods that might otherwise allow the growth of some undesirable microorganisms, and science is throwing new light on some of the safety mechanisms which keep these traditional foods safe.

It is sometimes recommended to freeze meat before use if it is to be used in the production of raw salami, to kill any parasites which may be present. A recent study * has shown that a salt level of 1.3%, combined with a pH of 5.2 or less, is able to inactivate the undesirable *Trichinella* in 24–28 hours. Complete inactivation of the parasite was seen after 7–10 days.

The rapid acidification results in a slightly sour taste which will stand up to the strong flavours of the chilli and other spices. It is possible to adjust, or even substitute, the spices used to flavour the salami, but the sugar and salt should not be reduced as this may impact negatively upon the safety of the cured meat.

The salami can be tied off in longer lengths, if preferred, of up to around 30cm/12in, or shorter lengths of approximately 10cm/4in.

* REFERENCE D.E. Hill, J. Luchansky, A. Porto-Fett, H.R. Gamble, V.M. Fournet, D.S. Hawkins-Cooper, A.A. Gajadhar, R. Holley, V.K. Juneja, J.P. Dubey, Curing conditions to inactivate Trichinella spiralis muscle larvae in ready-to-eat pork sausage, Food and Waterborne Parasitology, Volumes 6–7, 2017, Pages 1-8, ISSN 2405-6766, https://doi.org/10.1016/j.fawpar.2017.06.001. (http://www.sciencedirect.com/science/article/pii/S2405676616300208)

INGREDIENTS

Pork shoulder, weighing 450g/1lb

Pork belly, weighing 250g/9oz

0.2g LS25 (or similar fast-acting Starter culture used as per manufacturer's instructions)

Curing Salt #2, 2.5g/¹⁄₁₆oz per 1 kg/2.2lb of meat, optional (this must be measured accurately for the exact quantity of meat being used; see the notes on curing salts on pages 16–19 and always follow the manufacturer's instructions)

18g/²⁄₃oz pure dried vacuum (PDV) salt

8g/¼oz dextrose or sugar

2.5ml/½ tsp ground white pepper

1.5ml/¼ tsp garlic powder or 1–2 cloves of crushed garlic

1.5–2.5ml/¼–½ tsp dried chilli flakes

1.5ml/¼ tsp ground coriander

Natural hog casing

FAST FERMENTATION

The salami is piped into a natural hog casing, the small diameter of which will aid drying, resulting in a faster-cured sausage which is ready to enjoy in less than 2 weeks.

1 Soak the natural casing in water for 2 hours to soften it before filling.

2 Weigh the pork shoulder and belly, and chop them into evenly-sized chunks small enough to fit into the mincer. Placing the meat in the freezer for 5–10 minutes before mincing it will make it firmer.

3 Mince the pork belly and shoulder through a 3–5mm/⅛–¼in plate into a small bowl. Alternate each meat type as this will make it easier to mix.

4 Unless the manufacturer's instructions indicate otherwise, dissolve the starter culture in a tablespoon of water and sprinkle it over the meat. Mix it in well to ensure even distribution. Weigh the curing salt accurately if using. Add it to the PDV salt and make sure they are thoroughly mixed. Mix the salt(s) into the meat carefully to ensure an even distribution.

5 Add the dextrose or sugar to the meat along with the white pepper, garlic or garlic powder, chilli flakes and ground coriander. Mix well; the salami can be spoiled by inadequate mixing at this stage.

6 Pack the salami mixture into a sausage stuffer. Try to avoid trapping air in the mixture, which can be caused by packing it loosely. It is also possible to use the filling nozzle on your mincer to fill the casings.

7 Reserve a sample tablespoon of the mixture, to monitor pH development over the following 2 days. Check it with a pH meter or pH papers. It is essential to keep this sample at the same temperature as the salami so that the reading is a reliable indicator.

8 Place the casing over the end of the nozzle, making sure that the tip reaches the tied end of it. Crank the handle to begin filling; working slowly but steadily to avoid incorporating too much air and, if using natural casing, to avoid overfilling.

9 Squeeze the meat down to the end of the casing. Push out the air and seal the end of the casing. For natural casings, simply tie a knot near to the top of the salami filling.

10 Leave the salami in a warm place, no lower than 24–28°C/75–82°F. The fermentation will take up to 2 days. The fermentation will proceed more quickly at higher temperatures. Hang the salami in a plastic box, which can make an acceptable fermentation chamber and will help to maintain a high level of humidity. Monitor the acidity development of the sample during this time. When checked, at the end of the fermentation the pH must reach 5.00 or lower, but the salami may begin to taste very sour if the pH drops below 4.60.

11 Once the target acidity has been reached, the salami should be hung to dry at 15–16°C/59–61°F for 10 days. Relative humidity during drying should ideally be around 75%. The salami can be enjoyed after this short drying period.

TO SERVE Peel back the fibrous casing as far as you intend to slice the salami and cut it with a very sharp knife. The cut face can be covered with clingfilm or food wrap to stop it drying.

11

VENISON SALAMI

Venison, or deer meat, is full-flavoured but, being naturally very lean, it needs the addition of some pork fat to give a softer mouthfeel in the salami. This recipe uses the rich flavours of juniper to enhance the taste of the venison.

Like the salami piccante, this recipe is a fast fermentation using a rapid-acting starter culture to acidify the meat. As well as the starter culture, you must make sure that the correct temperature is held throughout the fermentation.

Venison can be highly variable in taste. This reflects the different species of deer which are marketed under the name, as well as differences between wild and farmed meat. Wild deer may be more active than their farmed equivalent, so the meat can be tougher and leaner. The meat from younger deer will be more tender than from older animals and the venison obtained from a doe, or female deer, is less tough than that of the male.

It is not altogether easy to describe the flavour of the different species of wild deer in comparative terms. Sex and age of the animal, season and conditions of harvesting and hanging all have an impact on flavour and texture, often making such comparisons meaningless. Several species of deer are farmed for meat. Red deer is quite common, but you may also be able to find the meat of the fallow deer, which can have quite a fine texture and good flavour. Sika deer can sometimes have a stronger flavour while the meat of the Muntjac is occasionally described as tasting like lamb.

The meat should be hung for a short time only, to avoid the 'gamey' flavours that can sometimes put people off. Warm temperatures during hanging will also cause the meat to become very strong-tasting and if there is a significant period between shooting a wild deer and hanging it, then this can cause the meat to spoil more rapidly. Keeping the carcass, and meat that is butchered from it, under refrigerated conditions as soon as possible after slaughter will avoid these very strong flavours and will help to avoid the growth of harmful bacteria.

The cut of meat will also impact upon the texture of the final salami. Here I recommend saddle, which is one of the best tender cuts, taken from the back. You could also use haunch (back leg) though it is tougher. Shoulder cuts would be tougher still. As a rule, the older the animal the more tender the cut from it you should use.

While there is usually only a little fat on deer meat, it will tend to have a much stronger flavour than that of the lean meat and you may wish to trim it off.

Follow the simple instructions on food safety on pages 34–35. It is important to use a whole cut of meat and mince it yourself rather than buying pre-minced venison. You should freeze the venison for several days prior to mincing it, especially when it is wild rather than farmed. You may also wish to 'sear and shave' the meat (see page 67) to further reduce the likelihood of pathogenic *E. coli* contaminating the salami.

Venison saddle or haunch, weighing 450g/1lb

Pork backfat, weighing 250g/9oz

0.2g LS25 (or similar fast-acting Starter culture used as per manufacturer's instructions)

18g/⅔oz pure dried vacuum (PDV) salt

Curing Salt #2, 2.5g/¹⁄₁₆oz per 1 kg/2.2lb of meat, optional (this must be measured accurately for the exact quantity of meat being used; see the notes on curing salts on pages 16–19 and always follow the manufacturer's instructions)

5ml/1 tsp juniper berries, crushed

8g/¼oz dextrose or sugar

2.5ml/½ tsp ground black pepper

1.5ml/¼ tsp garlic powder or 1–2 cloves of crushed garlic

1.5ml/¼ tsp grated nutmeg

Natural hog casing

STARTER CULTURE

It is important in this recipe to make sure that the starter culture is able to ferment the type of sugar that you plan to use. Glucose and sucrose are commonly used and many of the commercial starter cultures can ferment both these sugars.

1 Soak the natural casing in water for 2 hours before filling them.

2 Weigh the venison and chop the meat into even-sized chunks. These chunks should be small enough to fit into the mincer. If you like, placing the chopped meat in the freezer for 5–10 minutes before you start mincing can make it easier as it will be a little firmer.

3 Chop the pork backfat into rough cubes of up to 1cm/½in.

4 Mince the venison through a 3–5mm/⅛–¼in plate into a small bowl. Mix the backfat cubes into the minced venison.

5 Dissolve the fast-acting starter culture into a tablespoon of water and sprinkle it over the meat. Mix it in well to ensure even distribution.

6 Carefully weigh the PDV salt and the curing salt if using, and mix them together very well. Mix the salt(s) into the meat very thoroughly to ensure even distribution.

7 Grind the juniper berries using a pestle and mortar and add them to the meat along with the sugar, black pepper, garlic, and grated nutmeg.

8 Mix all the ingredients together very well for several minutes, to ensure everything is evenly distributed.

9 Pack the venison salami mixture tightly into a sausage stuffer and avoid trapping air in it. Alternatively use the filling nozzle on your mincer to fill the casings instead of the stuffer.

10 Place the casing over the end of the nozzle, making sure that the tip reaches the tied end of it. Crank the handle to begin filling; work slowly but steadily to avoid incorporating too much air into the casing and, if using natural casings, to avoid overfilling.

11 Reserve a sample tablespoon of the mixture, to monitor pH development at several points over the following 2 days. Check it with a pH meter or pH papers. It is essential to keep this sample at the same temperature as the salami so that the reading is a reliable indicator of the fermenting sausages.

12 Squeeze the meat down to the end of the casing. Push out the air and seal the end of the casing. For natural casings, simply tie a knot near to the top of the salami filling. Weigh the salami and record the weight.

13 Leave the salami in a warm place, at a temperature no lower than 28°C/82°F. The acidification should take 2 days at most but will proceed more quickly at higher temperatures. Hang the venison salami in a plastic box (see Equipment on page 27), which can make an acceptable fermentation chamber and will help to maintain a high level of humidity. Monitor the acidity development during this time; it must reach pH 5.00 or lower by the end of the fermentation.

14 After fermentation, the salami should be hung to dry at 15–16°C/59–61°F for about 10 days at a relative humidity of around 75%. The salami can be enjoyed after this short drying period, or dried for longer if you prefer, until it loses 30% of its initial weight.

TO SERVE Peel back the fibrous casing and cut the salami into thin rounds using a very sharp knife. The cut face can be covered with clingfilm or food wrap to stop it drying. I like to serve venison salami with a rich red wine, possibly a fruity and slightly spicy Syrah.

CHORIZO

Infused with the flavour and colour of paprika, this classic cured meat brings a taste of Spain to the charcuterie platter but can also pep-up scrambled eggs and rich tomato and bean stews.

Pronounced chor-eee-tho, or even chor-eee-so, rather than cho-ritz-o, there is very little difference between the process steps used in the preparation of the Milano- and Toscano-style salamis (pages 68 and 76) and those of this cured sausage. The flavour profile, however, is quite different, reflecting its origin in the Iberian Peninsula and the Moorish influences on the food of that region. The sweet, aniseed flavours of fennel and the gentle heat of black pepper are abandoned in favour of subtle smokiness, gentle spiciness and intense colour.

There are two variations on the basic chorizo recipe – Sobrasada, a soft, spreadable meat paste from the Balearic Islands, lying in the Mediterranean Sea off the east coast of Spain, and Chorizo Parrilla, which is a type of 'cooking chorizo' which should be grilled rather than air-dried. The recipe for Sobrasada can be found on page 100 while the Parrilla is prepared by mixing chorizo spices into a plain pork sausage mix (such as the one on page 156).

For those of you who like to see larger chunks of fat in their chorizo to contrast against the rich orange-red of the meat, reserve some pork fat before mincing and, instead, chop it finely before adding it to the rest of the ingredients.

For a simple and satisfying supper, finely slice some onion, garlic and red pepper and gently fry them in a little olive oil until soft. Add some sliced chorizo and a cupful of soaked, cooked and drained chickpeas. Pour in just enough passata (strained tomato sauce) to coat the chickpeas without drowning them and allow the sauce to thicken for a minute whilst stirring. Season to taste and serve with grated 'cured' or old Manchego or sheep's cheese.

INGREDIENTS

Pork shoulder, weighing 700g/1lb 9oz

Pork fat, weighing 300g/10½oz

0.5g Bactoferm T-SPX salami starter culture (or similar slow-acidifying culture according to manufacturer's instructions)

Curing Salt #2, 2.5g/¹⁄₁₆oz per 1 kg/2.2lb of meat, optional (this must be measured accurately for the exact quantity of meat being used; see the notes on curing salts on pages 16–19 and always follow the manufacturer's instructions)

27g/1oz pure dried vacuum (PDV) salt

2g/¹⁄₁₆oz sugar

2.5ml/½ tsp ground black pepper

2.5ml/½ tsp garlic powder

5–15ml/1–3 tsp hot smoked paprika or a mixture of hot and sweet smoked paprika, according to taste

Natural hog casing

1 Soak the fibrous salami casing in water while preparing the filling for the chorizo. It should be soaked for at least half an hour.

2 Weigh the pork shoulder and fat, chopping the meat into evenly-sized chunks that are small enough to fit into the mincer. To make the meat easier to handle, it can be placed in the freezer for 10 minutes before mincing it. Mince the meat through a 3–5mm/⅛–¼in plate into a small bowl. Mince a little of each of the ingredients in turn as this will make it easier to mix.

3 Dissolve the starter culture into a tablespoon of water. Sprinkle it over the meat.

4 Weigh the curing salt carefully, add it to the PDV salt and mix it very well. Add the salt mixture to the meat along with the sugar, black pepper, garlic powder and smoked paprika, mixing all the ingredients together well to ensure that the salt is evenly distributed.

5 Pack the well-mixed salami ingredients into a sausage stuffer or use the filling nozzle on your mincer. Place the casing over the end of the nozzle, making sure that the tip reaches the tied end. Crank the handle to begin filling, working slowly but steadily to avoid incorporating too much air. Reserve a sample tablespoon of the mixture to monitor pH development; there is usually a suitable quantity of the filling left in the nozzle of the stuffer.

6 Squeeze the meat down to the end of the casing. Push out the air and tie the end tightly with a length

of butcher's string, securing it with a double knot. Weigh the salami and record the weight. You will need it to calculate weight loss during drying.

7 Leave the chorizo in a warm, slightly humid room (preferably 24–26°C/75.2–78.8°F) for the period specified in the table on page 67. Monitor the sample temperature throughout – it should be kept relatively stable. When checked, the pH should reach 5.30 or less at the end of fermentation.

8 Once the fermentation is complete, hang the salami at 12–15°C/53.6–59°F until it loses around 30% of its initial weight. This may take a couple of months depending on the diameter of casing used and the relative humidity during drying – which should be maintained around 85% at first, falling to 70–75% after several weeks. If conditions are too dry, the casing may harden which can trap moisture at the core of the chorizo causing it to spoil. The humidity should not be too high either; at over 90% the chorizo will be likely to develop patches of unsightly rogue moulds. Rub any moulds which do appear with olive oil before they grow and produce spores. Once the salami has lost 30% of its initial weight, it can be served.

TO SERVE Peel back the casing as far as you intend to slice the salami and cut it with a very sharp knife or an electric meat slicer. The cut face can be covered with clingfilm or food wrap to stop it drying.

SOBRASADA

This spreadable chorizo originates in the Balearic Islands of Majorca, Menorca and Ibiza and its origin is often attributed to the high humidity of the islands which would have made curing the meat quite difficult.

To make sobrasada, the slow salami starter culture specified in the recipe should be swapped for a faster starter, such as Christian Hansen Bactoferm F-LC, which will provide positive competition to the growth of any harmful bacteria. Due to the short curing time, the risks involved in making this product are slightly increased so use meat from a reputable source, taken from a large cut, and ensure that the mincer and other equipment are spotlessly clean. It is strongly recommended that curing salts are used, according to the supplier's dosage instructions, in the preparation of sobrasada.

The other process steps are largely unchanged from that of the chorizo, however the incubation temperature is warmer; after filling the salami casings, incubate the sobrasada at 28°C/82.4°F for 2 days. The pH should decrease and the salami will typically smell and taste sour or 'tangy' compared to the slow-fermented, air-dried chorizo.

After incubating the sobrasada, it should be cured for a short period of time, typically a week or longer. Hang the sobrasada at 12–15°C/53.6-59°F while it dries. It should still be a slightly soft and almost-spreadable like pâté. Serve it with crusty bread.

KIELBASA

Originating in Poland, kielbasa is a variety of fermented dried sausages which are sometimes smoked to impart their characteristic flavour. This version takes inspiration from the Polish kielbasa but is a softer type of dried sausage, made using a fast fermentation that is followed by a short period of smoking and drying. It makes a delicious snack to enjoy with beer and cheese.

There are several different types of sausage available in Poland though the kabanos is perhaps the best known. This is a small stick of cured pork often served cold as a snack. It is usually hot-smoked at around 45°C/113°F for about an hour before being finished at a warmer temperature to cook the centre to a temperature of 71°C/160°F.

A dry sausage, kabanos should snap when they are bent. Mysliwska, or hunter's sausage, is another smoked and dried sausage, sometimes flavoured with juniper berries, and sometimes containing other meats in addition to pork. Krakowska is a highly seasoned wide-diameter slicing sausage, while the 'country-style' wiejska is a U-shaped sausage, flavoured with garlic.

With only salt and pepper used as seasoning, this kielbasa recipe relies on the meaty flavour of the pork, overlaid with subtle smokiness. The flavour is enhanced with a little smoked paprika rubbed into the casing.

This sausage will be cold-smoked rather than hot-smoked, then air-dried for a short time. Here, the cold smoke is employed largely to provide flavour.

Longer smoking and drying times would result in a firmer-textured sausage as it will allow more moisture to be lost.

This recipe is cold-smoked, using Curing Salt #2; some Polish sausages are hot-smoked and for this, Curing Salt #1 should be used instead. For more information on smoking see pages 225–226.

The recipe calls for pork shoulder. Choose pork with a good marbling of fat, which should make up around 20% of the meat. Where there is a greater proportion of lean meat, consider replacing some of the shoulder with a fattier cut, such as pork belly. Follow the instructions on food safety on pages 34–35, and always use a whole cut to prepare this dried sausage rather than pre-minced meat. You may wish to freeze the pork for several days prior to preparing it. Even with the fast fermentation and positive microbial competition from the starter cultures, you should make sure that all the equipment used is properly cleaned and disinfected before following this recipe.

The narrow diameter of the sausage allows it to dry quickly, and sheep casings under 2cm/¾in diameter are well suited to the recipe. Sheep casings can be quite delicate, so be careful when filling the sausage as overfilling can cause them to split easily. Hog casings by comparison are easier to work with.

Pork shoulder with a good layer of fat, weighing 600g/1lb 3oz

0.2g LS25 (or similar fast-acting Starter culture used as per manufacturer's instructions)

20g/¾oz pure dried vacuum (PDV) salt

Curing Salt #2, 2.5g/¹⁄₁₆ oz per 1 kg/2.2lb of meat, optional (this must be measured accurately for the exact quantity of meat being used; see the notes on curing salts on pages 16–19 and always follow the manufacturer's instructions)

8g/¼oz dextrose or sugar

2.5ml/½ tsp ground black pepper

5ml/1 tsp smoked paprika

Narrow-diameter natural sheep or hog casings

1 First, soak the natural casing in water. This should be done at least 2 hours before filling them.

2 Weigh out the pork shoulder and chop into chunks small enough to fit into the mincer. Place the meat pieces in the freezer for 5 minutes before mincing as it will make them easier to handle.

3 Mince the pork shoulder through a 3–5mm/⅛–¼in plate, collecting the minced meat in a bowl.

4 Unless the manufacturer's instructions indicate otherwise, dissolve the starter culture into a tablespoon of water and mix it thoroughly into the meat to ensure even distribution.

3

5 Weigh the PDV salt, recalculating the quantity if more meat was used than is specified in the recipe. If using the curing salt, weigh it out carefully and mix it with the ordinary salt. Pour the salt onto the meat and mix it in very well. This is important, as an uneven salt distribution will cause the kielbasa to spoil.

6 Add the sugar to the meat along with the black pepper and mix them in very well.

7 Pack the meat mixture into a sausage stuffer, or filling nozzle of your mincer, making sure that as little air as possible is trapped in it.

8 Feed the length of a pre-soaked natural casing over the end of the nozzle. Once it reaches the end, tie a knot in the casing to retain the meat. Crank the handle slowly but steadily to begin filling the casing. Take particular care if using sheep's casings as they break easily. The mixture will fill a few sausages around 25–30cm/10–12in long.

9 Reserve a sample spoonful of the kielbasa mixture. This should be kept in the same place and at the same temperature as the fermenting kielbasa sausage and will be used to regularly check the acidity development of the meat. Use a calibrated pH probe or pH papers.

10 Squeeze the meat down to the end of the casing. Push out the air and seal the end of the casing. For natural casings, simply tie a knot near to the top of the salami filling.

11 Hang the salami in a warm place, at 28°C/82°F. The fermentation will take up to 2 days but will proceed more quickly at higher temperatures. A plastic box can make a good fermentation chamber, allowing a high humidity to be held, keeping in heat and excluding pests such as flying insects. Monitor the acidity development during the fermentation, using the spoonful of mixture that was reserved. The salami should reach a pH of 5.00 or lower by the end of the fermentation.

12 After the fermentation is complete, rub the smoked paprika onto the outside of the sausage. This will help to provide colour and flavour. Weigh the kielbasa and record the weight to calculate moisture loss later. Hang the sausage in a cold smoker for up to 4 hours to impart a subtle smokiness. A smoking chamber can be easily assembled using a cold smoke generator (see page 32, and also 226).

13 Hang the salami to dry at 15–16°C/59–61°F for 10–20 days. The relative humidity during drying should be 75% and the kielbasa should lose around 35% of its weight during this time. The casing should shrink with the sausage.

TO SERVE Peel back the fibrous casing and cut the kielbasa into short pieces with a very sharp knife. The cut face can be covered with clingfilm or food wrap to stop it drying. The sausage makes a good bar snack with lager-style beers.

3

COOKED MEATS & PÂTÉS

This chapter covers charctuerie products which are cooked during their preparation. It includes a variety of cold-cuts, pâtés and terrines which can be made ahead of serving and chilled until needed. Cooked ham, salt beef, pastrami and Brussels pâté are covered here, as well as some more unusual recipes for pressed ox tongue, and the beautiful parsley-stuffed chine with its distinctive green stripes.

Some of the dishes are intended to be served hot and include confit duck as well as some traditional, warming dishes from the British Isles, such as haggis and faggots, the latter being a type of meatball made with liver. These recipes require little or no specialised equipment, beyond what may reasonably be found in the average home kitchen.

COOKED HAM

Cooked ham, such a ubiquitous item in your local supermarket, can be a real disappointment but this home-made version is packed with the flavour of traditionally cured ham.

This dish has its roots in the times when meat was heavily salted to preserve it, then rinsed before being cooked either by boiling, roasting or a combination of boiling and baking as is the case here. Leftover cooked meat would be kept in a cool storeroom or larder and brought out again for another meal.

It is important to use fresh (unsalted) pork rather than gammon, which is already cured, when preparing your ham. There can be some confusion over the terminology but the easiest way to remember it is that once pork leg has been salted, it is referred to as 'gammon', which takes its name from the old French *gambon*, referring to the leg or *gambe*. Once the gammon has been cooked it is often referred to as 'ham' which derives its name from similar roots (*jambon* from the French *jambe* or leg). The term 'ham' is also used for the air-dried leg on page 38. In some places the terms gammon and ham appear to be largely interchangeable; elsewhere, the term 'fresh ham' can indicate a pork leg that has not been salted.

All of these semantic issues aside, the flavour of the ham depends on two things – the quality of the meat used to make it, and the flavours added to the brine or to the rind during the final roasting. Prepare the brine a few days in advance to allow the flavours to diffuse before immersing the pork leg to infuse the warm flavour of the juniper.

INGREDIENTS

Half pork leg (or 'fresh ham'), weighing around 2kg/4lb 7oz

Brine made of 340g/12oz pure dried vacuum (PDV) salt in 3.78ltr/6.7pints/1 US gallon cold water

45ml/3 tbsp golden or brown sugar

2–3 bay leaves

10–12 juniper berries

15ml/1 tbsp black peppercorns

A small handful of fresh thyme

1 onion

1 carrot

2–3 sticks of celery

For the glaze:

2.5ml/½ tsp ground black pepper

15–30ml/1–2 tbsp honey

15–30ml/1–2 tbsp grain mustard or Dijon mustard

1 Make up the brine in a container such as a food-grade plastic tub which is large enough to hold both the brine and the meat.

2 Add the sugar, bay leaves, juniper, peppercorns and thyme to the brine and stir well. The brine should be kept in the refrigerator or cold larder. It can be used immediately or made up a day or so before it is needed to allow the flavours to infuse. Peel one whole onion and roughly quarter it. Peel a carrot and chop it into long chunks. Half the celery sticks lengthways down the centre and chop them into strips. Add the onion, carrot and celery to the brine.

3 Rinse the pork leg and place into the container with the brine. Place it in the refrigerator, maintaining the temperature at 3–5°C/37–41°F, and allow the ham to brine for 3–4 days.

4 After 3–4 days, remove the meat from the brine, which can be discarded along with the herbs and vegetables. The pork may feel firmer and may have changed colour slightly. Rinse the pork, or 'gammon'.

5 Put the pork in a pan of cold water, large enough to fit it completely. Bring it gently to the boil and then simmer over a low to medium heat until the leg is cooked through. The water should be topped up once or twice as the meat is cooking. This should take around 2–4 hours, allowing around 20 minutes per 500g/18 minutes per lb.

6 Remove the meat from the pan and discard the water. Preheat the oven to 200°C/392°F/Gas mark 6.

7 Place the ham on a roasting tray. If you prefer, you can trim off the rind using a sharp knife or score the fat to cut a criss-cross shape but do not cut into the muscle below. Mix the ground pepper, honey and mustard together to make a paste and apply it evenly to the outside of the ham. Don't cover the ham to the point that the glaze is running off; if any glaze remains, the ham can be 'topped up' with it partway through cooking.

8 Bake the ham in the oven for 10–15 minutes until the glaze sets of the surface and starts to brown. The meat should be left to rest for at least 15 minutes before serving. If not serving, place somewhere cool and transfer to the refrigerator as soon as possible.

CHOOSING A PORK CUT

The half pork leg may be from the shank end, which is the tapered cut of meat from just above the hock or from the upper half of the ham, near the rump. If using the upper half of the ham, any traces of the 'aitch' bone from the pelvis will need to be removed. If it is present, it will appear as a small square of bone attached at the hip joint. Ask your butcher to remove it or locate the ball of the hip joint and cut away the connective tissues linking it to the pelvis. The lower, shank end has the 'classic' ham shape. If you use a whole leg, the brining time may take up to 10 days.

LINCOLNSHIRE CHINE

This cooked pork hailing from one of the eastern counties of England makes a striking alternative to cooked ham. Lincolnshire stuffed chine is something of a rarity: chine is a regional dish which has been celebrated by the Slow Food movement but is hardly seen outside the county that it draws its name from. It is indeed worthy of celebration. Chine is a traditional English word for 'backbone' and this is a brine-cured pork back which is then cooked. The unusual thing about Lincolnshire chine is that, before cooking, several deep cuts are sliced into the flesh and packed with chopped parsley. When the meat is ready to serve, it is carved across the seams of stuffing to give each slice its distinctive pink and green stripes.

Stuffed chine is traditionally made with a cut of meat taken from the back of the pig, between the shoulders, though this tends to be harder to find these days. The bone provided stability, holding the chine together as it cooked. However it is possible to follow this recipe with other cuts of meat, such as the upper shoulder cut that I have used here, which is sometimes called a 'Boston butt' and which includes the cut that is sometimes referred to as 'pork collar'.

Chine is a substantial, robust food hailing from the very roots of British farmhouse cooking, a marriage of fat, acidity and generously-applied herbs. It is traditionally served with English mustard, and a drizzle of vinegar to cut through the fat. The meat dishes of Lincolnshire tend to be dominated by strong herb flavours – parsley in the case of chine, and sage in the case of the sausages on page 159.

INGREDIENTS

Pork shoulder or collar joint (sometimes described as a Boston butt), weighing approximately 3kg/6lb 10oz

Brine made of 400g/14oz pure dried vacuum (PDV) salt in 5.3ltr/9⅓pints/1.4 US gallons cold water

6–8 generous bunches of fresh parsley

A bunch of fresh thyme

1 Make up the brine in a container such as a food-grade plastic tub which is large enough to hold both the brine and the meat, and which will fit in the refrigerator.

2 Slash the pork in 3–5 parallel lines to create small pockets in the meat; do not cut all the way through.

3 Immerse the pork in the brine and place this in the refrigerator for 4 days, maintaining the temperature at 3–5°C/37–41°F. If the joint weighs more than 3kg/6lb 10oz, add an extra half-day for each additional 450g/1lb.

4 Turn the joint in the brine each day, stirring up any salt which has settled on the base as you do. The joint may shrink slightly, and it can be quite normal for the outside to darken slightly and feel firmer by the end of brining.

5 At the end of the brining time, take the meat out and wash off the brine using fresh water. While it can be common to find recipes which call for brined hams and similar cuts to be soaked in fresh water before cooking, this is not absolutely necessary unless the salt level is very high. If the recommended brining time has been exceeded, the joint may be soaked in fresh water for 10–30 minutes to rebalance it. If your chine sometimes turns out a little too salty, the original brining time can be reduced slightly, which would achieve the same purpose.

6 Using a chef's knife in a steady rocking action, chop the fresh parsley and thyme down into fine, evenly sized shreds as if preparing a garnish. Place the point of the knife on the chopping board and use it as an axis to rock the knife over the herb mixture. Turn the knife 90 degrees after each series of cuts to ensure that the pieces are evenly sized.

7 Generously pack the herb mixture into the pockets in the pork, pushing to force as much of it in as possible.

8 Wrap the chine tightly in muslin, knotting the top. The bag of chine should then be placed in a large pan of cold water, brought gently to the boil, and simmered over a low to medium heat for about 3–4 hours, during which time the internal temperature should exceed 80°C/176°F. The water should be topped up several times as the meat is cooking. Use boiling water from the kettle to do this so as not to cool the cooking meat when you add the extra water.

9 Remove the pan from the heat but do not remove the muslin bag yet and do not discard the water. Leave the pan and its contents to cool. If it is a warm day, the pan can be sat in a basin of cold water. After one hour or as soon as it is cool enough, transfer the contents of the pan to a bowl or tub in the fridge and leave it for two hours. The fat should harden in this time, you will see white particles in the liquid.

10 Once the meat has cooled, pour off the water and press the bag of meat under a plate for several hours. This will help the meat and stuffing to retain its shape during carving. Return it to the fridge while it is pressing.

11 Unwrap the meat and carve it against the seam of the stuffing. It is quite normal for the meat to fall apart slightly at the lines of stuffing. Use a very sharp knife in a gentle sawing action to avoid unnecessary damage to the slices.

TO SERVE Arrange the slices of chine on a plate and sprinkle a tiny amount of cider vinegar or wine vinegar over them. Serve with a spoonful of vivid yellow English mustard. For a simple summer lunch, slice generous slabs of the chine and serve with crusty bread, Cheddar cheese, pickled onion and a handful of washed salad leaves. A pint of ale makes a good match to wash it down.

The stuffed chine should be stored in the refrigerator and used up within a week.

SALT BEEF & PASTRAMI

Bring a touch of the New York deli to your kitchen with this delicious and tender beef brisket, which is cured and then prepared in one of two ways: boiled as salt beef, or coated with aromatic spices and steamed to make pastrami.

Salt beef is an incredible comfort food. The brisket's inviting pink colour and moist, slightly salty flavour have an almost universal appeal though its alternative name, corned beef, can sometimes conjure up less-appealing thoughts of canned meat.

True salt beef is also an essential ingredient in the 'Reuben', one of the classic sandwiches known across the world, featuring alongside rye bread, Emmental cheese, sauerkraut and Russian dressing, which is not very Russian at all, possibly having originated in America at the turn of the century. The Reuben is an incredible balance of savoury, sweet, salty, sour and umami flavours, which perhaps explains its enduring popularity. Salt beef has a natural affinity with mustard and pickled gherkins, and is delicious served in thick slabs in a beigel (or bagel), the world-famous bread ring which has its origins in the Jewish communities of Poland. The origins of salted beef itself is claimed by many, including Ireland.

Pastrami has also become a staple of the American deli counter, possibly arriving with immigrants from Eastern Europe in the late nineteenth and early twentieth centuries. With such international origins, it is perhaps unsurprising that both pastrami and salt beef found their natural spiritual home in the cultural melting pot that is New York City.

The two recipes start out in the same way, with the meat being dry-cured for several days. The salt beef is cooked as a rolled joint of meat, while the pastrami is opened out and coated with spices. Both processes involve slow cooking, in simmering water or steamed in the oven. This is done to break down some of the collagen in the connective tissue of the meat and turn it into gelatine. The soft texture of the meat depends on this breakdown during cooking so do not be tempted to turn up the oven to speed up the process, and do leave the meat to rest after cooking.

The curing salt will help to preserve an attractive red-pink colour in the meat. If you choose not to use the curing salt the meat will be darker, possibly with a greyer hue, once cooked. Curing Salt #1 is used in this recipe, as the meat is cooked after curing.

Alternatively, it is also possible to salt the meat by brining it. Larger rolled joints in particular, over 1kg/2lb 2oz, will take up the salt more efficiently if brined. To do this, the meat should be placed in a brine consisting of 340g/12oz salt mixed into 3.78ltr/6.7pints/1 US gallon of cold water. It is also possible to use a live brine, such as the Wiltshire cure (see brine-cured bacon on page 175), which contains an active microflora of bacteria that enhance flavour development and meat pigmentation. Make up the brine in a large, clean bowl, adding the sugar, bay leaves, juniper berries and peppercorns directly to the water. The brine can be used immediately but can be kept in the refrigerator and reused, so long as the salt level is topped up after each use.

SALT BEEF

1 rolled beef brisket, weighing approximately 1–1.5kg/2lb 2oz–3lb 3oz

Curing Salt #1, 2.5g/¹⁄₁₆ oz per 1 kg/2.2lb of meat, optional (see the notes on curing salts on pages 16–19 and always follow the manufacturer's instructions)

60g/2oz pure dried vacuum (PDV) salt

5–8 juniper berries

15ml/1 tbsp black peppercorns

20g/¾oz soft brown sugar

2–3 bay leaves

1–2 carrots, chopped, optional

¼–½ head of celery, chopped, optional

½ onion, chopped, optional

1 Weigh out the salt, adjusting the weight if the meat is more or less than the quantity specified. If using the curing salt, weigh it out carefully and stir it into the PDV salt, mixing it in well. Measure out and crush the juniper berries and peppercorns, adding them to the cure mixture along with the sugar and bay leaves.

2 Cut the strings tying the joint of brisket and unroll it, trimming off any excess fat or scraps of meat. The joint is unrolled to speed up the salting time, and larger rolled joints, over 1kg/2lb 2oz, will take up the salt more efficiently if brined.

3 Rinse the brisket and pat it dry with a kitchen towel. Rub the cure mixture evenly onto all sides of the meat.

4 Place the meat into a plastic zip-lock bag, large vacuum pouch or plastic tub. The brisket should be kept in the cure, in the refrigerator, at a temperature of 3–5°C/37–41°F and for about 5 days.

5 Once the meat has cured, remove it from the bag or tub. It is normal for it to feel firmer at this point, and to look darker especially if you haven't used curing salt.

6 Rinse the cure from the salted brisket by soaking in fresh water for a few minutes.

7 Re-roll and tie the joint of meat with string. Place the joint in a pan of clean water possibly with the addition of chopped carrot, celery and/or onion. Bring the pan to the boil. Reduce the heat immediately to the lowest setting and cover the pan with a lid. Cook the brisket for around 2–3 hours, until cooked through.

8 Once cooked, remove the salt beef from the pan and rest it for 10–15 minutes before carving into thick slices. The meat can be served warm but, once cooled, should be refrigerated until needed.

PASTRAMI

1 rolled beef brisket, weighing approximately 1–1.5kg/2lb 2oz–3lb 3oz

60g/2oz pure dried vacuum (PDV) salt

Curing Salt #1, 2.5g/¹⁄₁₆ oz per 1 kg/2.2lb of meat, optional (see the notes on curing salts on pages 16–19 and always follow the manufacturer's instructions)

20g/¾oz soft brown sugar

2–3 bay leaves

5–8 juniper berries

15ml/1 tbsp black peppercorns

5–10ml/1–2 tsp coriander seeds

5ml/1 tsp ground black pepper

2.5ml/½ tsp ground cinnamon

2.5ml/½ tsp garlic powder

1 Weigh out the PDV salt, adjusting the weight if the meat is more or less than the quantity specified. If using the curing salt, weigh it out carefully and stir it into the PDV salt, mixing it in well.

2 Cut the strings tying the joint and unroll it, trimming off any excess fat or scraps. Rinse and pat it dry with a kitchen towel. Cut the meat in halves and place in a zip-lock bag, vacuum pouch or plastic tub.

3 Add the salt mixture, sugar, bay leaves, juniper berries and whole peppercorns. The brisket should be kept in the cure, in the refrigerator, at a temperature of 3–5°C/37–41°F for about 2 days. Once the meat has cured, remove it from the bag or tub. It is normal for it to feel firmer at this point and to look darker.

4 Measure out the coriander and grind it roughly with a pestle and mortar. Mix together with the ground black pepper, cinnamon and garlic powder.

5 After removing the brisket from the brine, rinsing and drying it, rub the top of the meat with the spice mixture.

6 If you like, the pastrami can be placed for 2–3 hours in a cold smoker (see page 32). Alternatively, a little smoked paprika added to the spice mix can impart a subtle smoky flavour if you do not have the facility to smoke your meat.

7 Unless you have a steamer big enough to take it, place the pastrami on a rack in a deep roasting tray. Pour enough boiling water into the bottom of the tray to fill it to around 2cm/¾in deep.

8 Cover the tray with aluminium foil to enclose the pastrami. Fold the edges of the foil under the tray to secure it. Steam the pastrami in the oven for around 2 hours at 100–120°C/212–248°F until tender but not over-done. Once cooked, leave it to rest for 10–15 minutes or more, and refrigerate once cool.

TO SERVE The pastrami should be sliced into thin strips with a sharp knife and served cold, perhaps with rye bread, mustard and pickles.

PRESSED TONGUE

Tongue is an often-neglected cut of meat and there is no doubt that it isn't the prettiest recipe to prepare, but cooked slowly until tender its marbling of fat gives lots of succulence and savoury flavour, making it a delicious cold cut.

Some of the offal cuts and products have a lot of fat and collagen, which is a protein found in connective tissue. Given sufficient slow cooking, this collagen will break down to release gelatine. It also provides texture, while the fat carries a lot of the flavour. If overcooked however, the collagen will cause the meat to become tough and chewy.

Like brawn, a cold cut made from offcuts from the head of the pig or calf set in natural gelatine, the cooked tongue relies on the breakdown of the collagen into a jelly which will help to set the meat once cooled. Traditionally, cuts like this would have been placed into a small press, sometimes called a meat press or tongue press. This usually takes a round shape in order to mould the meat, and has a small screw press attached in order to provide pressure. This pressure is necessary to fuse the tongue, which is rolled up at the end of cooking. An alternative to the special press is employed in this recipe, where we make use of an ordinary bowl and a plate which fits easily inside it. The plate can be weighed down to provide the necessary pressure.

The curing salts are optional for this recipe but when used will help to keep a pink colour in the cooked tongue. A live brine, inoculated with nitrate-reducing bacteria such as the Wiltshire cure, would have a similar, if less pronounced effect. Curing Salt #1 is used here as the meat is cooked rather than air-dried. The flavour of the cooked tongue can be enhanced by additional ingredients either to the brine or the cooking liquor. Cloves work well but allspice, mustard seeds, star anise, mace and nutmeg also add flavour for those who wish to experiment.

INGREDIENTS

Ox tongue, weighing approximately 1.5kg/3lb 3oz

Brine made of 340g/12oz pure dried vacuum (PDV) salt in 3.78ltr/6.7pints/1 US gallon cold water

20g/¾oz soft brown sugar

2–3 bay leaves

4–5 cloves

15ml/1 tbsp black peppercorns

Curing Salt #1, 2.5g/¹⁄₁₆oz per 1 kg/2.2lb of meat, optional (see the notes on curing salts on pages 16–19 and always follow the manufacturer's instructions)

1 bouquet garni, made of a small bunch of thyme and bay leaf tied together

½ bunch of celery, chopped

1 carrot, chopped

5 garlic cloves, peeled but left whole

1 Make up the brine in a clean bowl, bucket, or large vacuum pouch. Add the sugar, bay leaves, cloves and peppercorns. Stir the brine well until the salt and sugar completely dissolve. If using the curing salt, weigh it out carefully and stir it into the brine. The curing salt is toxic in excess and the correct quantity must be used.

2 The brine can be kept in the refrigerator until needed or used immediately. Preparing it several days in advance will allow more time for flavours to infuse into the liquid – as will bringing it to the boil and immediately cooling it before use.

3 The tongue should be soaked in clean water to wash off any blood or dirt. The texture of the tongue is quite rough and you may need to scrub it well if it is particularly soiled.

4 Put the tongue in the brine to cure. It should be kept in the refrigerator at a temperature of 3–5°C/37–41°F and left to cure for 1 day.

5 Remove the meat from the brine the following day, and rinse it again. The tongue should then be placed in a pan of cold water, with the bouquet garni, celery, carrot and garlic cloves. The bouquet garni is made by tying a small bunch of fresh thyme and a bay leaf using some natural cotton string.

6 Bring the pan to the boil then turn down the heat and simmer gently for 3–3½ hours. The tongue should be soft enough for a skewer to slide into it easily. If there is resistance to the skewer then the tongue may have been over-cooked.

7 Once cooked, remove the tongue from the pan, reserving the cooking liquor. Cool the tongue in some cold water. When it is cool enough to handle, peel off all of the tough outer layer. This hard covering is yellow-white and may appear to be blistered. Neaten up the tongue by trimming off any loose scraps of meat from the edges.

8 Roll the tongue into a tight round and place it into a bowl that is just big enough to hold it. Pour in a small amount of the cooking liquor, just enough to surround but not cover the tongue.

9 Place a plate on top of the tongue to press it. A small weight can be placed on the plate. The tongue should be placed in the fridge overnight.

10 The following day, the tongue can be removed from the bowl. Discard the small quantity of liquid which may have formed around the meat, which should have set with a small amount of natural jelly surrounding it.

TO SERVE The meat should be sliced thinly at 90 degrees to the direction of the tongue. Served cold, it makes a good addition to a cold meat platter or a delicious sandwich filling on white crusty bread with a spoonful of horseradish or hot English mustard.

CONFIT DUCK LEGS

Confit duck is nothing more complicated than cooked duck legs preserved under a layer of fat, but this is a great standby dish to keep in the larder, allowing a simple but impressive supper to be prepared at very short notice.

The cost of portioned duck legs and breasts can make buying and roasting the whole bird a more attractive proposition. The carcass will release a lot of strong-smelling fat, and it is this fat which is used to cover the confit duck legs, excluding air and helping to preserve them. The recipe also works well with other fatty poultry such as goose.

Many recipes for confit duck involve carving the uncooked carcass and cooking the legs in a pan of fat on the stove, before potting it. The recipe in this book makes use of the fat that is naturally released from the meat as it is roasting, and as it is roasted the meat becomes a little drier which will also help to preserve it. It is important to cook the meat slowly, but also to not overcook the duck, as the confit would be very tough if you did. The breast should still be pink when served to ensure that the confit has the desired melt-in-the-mouth texture.

The fat that is rendered from the carcass covers the cooked duck legs which will enable them to be stored for several weeks. After opening a jar of confit duck, I often retain the fat and use it to roast potatoes for another meal. This confit duck recipe is a gift that keeps on giving.

It may be necessary to top up the jar with additional rendered fat, with lard for example, if there is not enough duck fat to cover the meat in the jar. This should be fresh, as old fat can develop oxidised or rancid flavours, even when it is stored in a cool place away from light.

This recipe calls for fleur de sel, which are delicate and irregular sea salt crystals, harvested by hand from the surface of a salt pan as the water starts to evaporate. Ordinary pure dried vacuum salt can be used instead if this is not available. Coarse salt would be much slower to dissolve and is not suitable.

INGREDIENTS

One whole duck, weighing approximately 2kg/4lb 7oz

75g/2½oz fleur de sel (sea salt)

5ml/1 tsp garlic powder or several cloves, crushed

10ml/2 tsp ground black pepper

A small bunch of fresh thyme

A small bunch of fresh rosemary

Additional duck or goose fat (or lard) if necessary

1 First prepare the duck. Check the cavity of the duck and remove the giblets if they are present. The giblets are the offal of the duck and include the neck, heart, liver and gizzard, and are sometimes removed then placed within the bird's cavity in a plastic bag. You must remove this before cooking.

2 Rub the salt onto the skin of the duck, along with the garlic, black pepper and thyme leaves (strip the leaves from the thyme by running your fingers along the stalks from the tip downwards). Place a few sprigs of rosemary in the cavity. Cover the duck with clingfilm or food wrap, and place it in the refrigerator overnight to allow the salt and flavours to be taken up into the bird.

3 Remove the duck from the refrigerator and place it onto a rack over a roasting tray an hour before cooking to allow the meat to lose some of its chill. Preheat the oven to 120°C/248°F. Place the duck into the oven and cook for 2½–3 hours. The duck should be covered with aluminium foil for the first part of the cooking and removed for the final hour. Baste the duck by pouring some of the fat from the roasting tray back over the flesh once or twice during cooking to help to keep the meat moist. Do not open the oven door more than is absolutely necessary as doing so will cause the moist air to escape and can cause the duck to become very dry.

4 Once the duck is cooked, the juices should run clear when checked with a skewer. Remove the duck from the oven and allow the meat to rest for 10 minutes.

5 Carefully carve the duck, removing the legs. The breasts and wings can be enjoyed immediately, while the legs are used to prepare the confit.

6 The legs should be placed into a clean jar, just big enough to hold them.

7 Carefully sieve the molten duck fat into the jar, making sure that you do not include the water-based cooking juices which will be underneath the layer of fat. If there is not enough duck fat to cover the legs then melt some extra lard, or duck or goose fat. It is important to ensure that the legs are completely covered and are submerged below the surface of the fat. This should be approximately 2cm/¾in deep. Tap the jar gently on the work surface several times to release any air pockets as these could cause the meat to spoil.

8 Place the lid on the jar while the fat is still warm and leave it to cool. It should be stored in the refrigerator once cool enough and can be kept for up to one month. This confit duck recipe is not suitable for storage at ambient temperatures.

TO SERVE the confit duck, remove it from the jar. The excess fat can be scraped off and the confit can be roasted for 20 minutes at 180°C/356°F, or the duck and fat can be placed into a saucepan and gently heated together. This may take around 10–15 minutes until the leg is piping hot throughout. Serve the confit with mashed potatoes or puy lentils. Alternatively, for a delicious summer lunch, the confit is excellent shredded in a salad.

PÂTÉ

Delicious rich-tasting pâté spread on freshly toasted bread makes a simple supper, a rustic lunch or a tasty starter, and making your own could not be easier.

Pâté is one of the ultimate thrifty charcuterie products, making use of offal cuts, such as liver, that cannot be cured and dried. Instead the pâté is cooked to preserve it, and should then be stored in the refrigerator once it has been prepared as it spoils easily. While it is both nutritious and tasty, the offal does not last long as a preserved meat. Many shop-bought pâtés often have a relatively long expiry date on them, but this may rely on high levels of salt or other preservatives. Home-made pâté has a shorter shelf-life by comparison.

Liver is full of nutrients and is rich in protein, vitamins and minerals, including iron. Given how easy it is to prepare, it often surprises me that more people do not make their own pâté. Here the flavourings are quite subtle, depending on garlic, salt, pepper, a little sherry, some rich and creamy butter, and of course the flavour of the livers, which should be as fresh as possible.

The smooth chicken liver pâté is made by cooking the livers in a pan and then puréeing them using a food processor or stick blender. The Brussels-style pâté is made from pork liver and is puréed to a smooth consistency before cooking. Coarser varieties, such as Ardennes pâté, are often made using pig's liver with belly or shoulder meat, and puréed in a food processor before cooking. Sometimes a little finely chopped bacon will be added to the meat mixture, which is then cooked in a terrine dish or loaf tin, sitting in a tray of water in the oven. The recipe for this coarser type of Ardennes pâté is included in the terrine recipe as the method of preparing it is the same (see page 141).

For those of you who wish to experiment with different flavours in your pâté, I have included a recipe for a Provençal-style variation, with all the warm flavours of the south of France. It is also possible to experiment with other herbs and spices to create your own flavoured pâtés.

PICKLED GHERKINS

Pickled gherkins or cornichons make a great accompaniment to pâté. Sterilise some lidded jars in boiling water and allow to cool. Wash small, fresh cucumbers and pack them tightly into the jar. To make the brine, measure equal quantities of water and vinegar (minimum 5% acetic acid). Add 30g/1oz salt and about 15g/½oz sugar per litre (1.75pints/2 US pints) and bring to the boil. Pour the hot brine over the gherkins and seal the jars, filling right to the top. Allow the air bubbles to rise for a few minutes then top up the brine and seal the jar. Store in a cool dark place for 6 weeks.

CHICKEN LIVER PÂTÉ

Chicken livers, 500g/1lb 1oz

300ml/11fl oz milk

80g/3oz butter

2–3 garlic cloves, peeled and chopped in half

30ml/2 tbsp sherry or marsala wine

1.5ml/¼ tsp salt

1.5ml/¼ tsp ground white pepper

60g/2oz clarified butter, melted, optional for topping

1 Place the chicken livers into a clean bowl and pour in enough of the milk to just cover them. Soak the chicken livers in the milk for up to 6 hours in the refrigerator before making the pâté. Soaking is sometimes done to remove bitter and metallic flavours from the liver, and the milk will help to draw out some of the blood. The milk will turn pink whilst the livers are soaking; this should not be used afterwards and must be discarded.

2 Heat a large frying pan over a medium heat and add the butter and the garlic. Drain off the livers, chop them in half and add them to the pan.

3 Fry the livers gently over a medium heat, moving and turning them frequently to avoid burning them. They should be fried for around 5–10 minutes until golden and cooked through to the centre. Check them by cutting into one of the larger pieces.

4 Transfer the cooked livers to a clean bowl and leave them to cool for 5 minutes. Using a hand blender or food processor, purée the chicken livers until they form a smooth paste.

5 Pour in the sherry and stir the mixture well. If necessary, blend it again using the hand blender to incorporate the sherry into the paste.

6 Add the salt and pepper and stir it in to ensure that the seasonings are well mixed in. Transfer the paste into a dish or ramekins, pushing it down into the base and smoothing over the top with a knife.

TO SERVE The pâté can be eaten shortly after it has cooled, or it can be left in the fridge for a day or two to allow the flavour to develop. Serve with toast. Little cornichons or gherkins make a great accompaniment as their acidity helps to cut through the pâté's richness.

PROVENCAL-STYLE PÂTÉ

This recipe follows the smooth chicken liver pâté, but with some extra ingredients. Add 1.5m/¼ tsp of both dried thyme and dried oregano to the chicken livers before frying them. Finely chop half a red bell pepper and 2 shallots into small cubes, and fry in a little olive oil over a low heat until they are soft. This can be done while the cooked livers are cooling. Also chop 6 green pitted, brined olives into cubes of a similar size to the pepper and shallot. After puréeing the livers, stir in the chopped olives, fried peppers and shallots before transferring the mixture to the ramekins.

BRUSSELS-STYLE PÂTÉ

Pork livers, weighing 500g/1lb 1oz

300ml/11fl oz milk

30ml/2 tbsp sherry or marsala wine

80g/3oz butter, softened or melted

3 garlic cloves, peeled and chopped in half

1.5ml/¼ tsp salt

1.5ml/¼ tsp ground white pepper

60g/2oz clarified butter, melted, optional for topping

1 Place the livers into a clean bowl and pour in enough of the milk to just cover it. Soaking helps to remove bitter flavours from the liver. It should be soaked for up to 6 hours before making the pâté, and the milk should be discarded afterwards.

2 Drain the liver and place it in a food processor. Add the sherry, butter, garlic, salt and pepper. Purée the liver until it is reduced to a smooth paste.

3 Transfer the paste into some ramekins or small ovenproof dishes. The mixture should be pushed down into the base and the top should be smoothed over with a knife.

4 Preheat the oven to 150°C/300°F/Gas mark 2. Place the ramekins into a larger dish. Pour enough water into the larger dish for it to reach most of the way up the side of the ramekins. Cover the dish with aluminium foil, or a lid, and cook in the oven for 30 minutes until the liver is cooked through.

5 Leave the pâté to cool. It can be finished by pouring a little melted, clarified butter onto the top. Once cool enough, place in the refrigerator.

CLARIFIED BUTTER

Clarifying is the process of melting butter to evaporate off the moisture. Heat some butter gently in a pan; it will start to spit and bubble but continue until the bubbles just subside. Strain the oily butter, discarding the browned milk solids left at the bottom.

TERRINE

Terrines, with their coarse and meaty texture, are pleasantly rustic in style but, finished with a coat of bacon or Parma ham, they can make an elegant and sophisticated starter or a pleasing addition to a cold meat platter.

The terrine is made in much the same way as coarse pâté but, with the liver omitted, it has a far meatier flavour and texture. This recipe makes use of pork shoulder, which has a good mix of fat and lean meat, as well as some fattier pork belly to provide flavour. It is also possible to make the terrine with chicken, when the anise flavours of dried tarragon work very well as an addition to the thyme and oregano. Simply replace both the pork shoulder and belly with an equal quantity of chicken breast meat.

A recipe for an Ardennes-style pâté has also been included here, which requires only some minor changes to the basic recipe to make a terrine. Unlike the smooth Brussels-style pâté described on page 136, the meat is put though the food processor before it is cooked rather than afterwards. It is not chopped as finely, and the slightly uneven texture carries through to the finished terrine. It should be pleasantly chunky. The terrine is cooked in the oven in a loaf tin or dish sat in a bain-marie of water, made by filling a larger dish or roasting tray with water. This will help to ensure that the terrine is cooked through but stop it drying out.

As the terrine is a large dish, filled with ground-up meat, it is important to check the internal temperature at the end of cooking.

PORK TERRINE

Pork shoulder, weighing 800g/1lb 12oz

Pork belly, weighing 200g/7oz

2 garlic cloves, peeled and crushed

45ml/3 tbsp sherry

1.5ml/¼ tsp dried thyme

1.5ml/¼ tsp dried oregano

1.5ml/¼ tsp salt

1.5ml/¼ tsp ground black pepper

400g/14oz unsmoked streaky or side bacon (or finely sliced Parma ham)

200g/7oz cornichons (small gherkins)

1 First chop the pork shoulder and belly into rough cubes, to make it easier to cut them in the food processor.

2 Put half of the chopped shoulder and half of the belly into the food processor. Add the garlic, sherry, herbs, salt and pepper.

3 Pulse the control a few times to begin breaking the meat into smaller pieces, before 'blitzing' it for 1–2 minutes on full power until the meat forms a smooth purée.

4 Add the remaining half of the meat and switch the processor back on until the larger chunks have broken down slightly. The meat mixture should look fairly uneven and even a little lumpy at the end.

5 Line a loaf tin or terrine dish with the bacon (or Parma ham), ensuring that each slice overlaps the last and leaving enough bacon hanging over the edge of the tin to be able to cover the top of the terrine after it has been filled. Add half of the meat mixture, pushing it down into the base of the tin.

6 Lay the baby gherkins in rows on the surface of the meat in the tin. Their longest side should be lined up with the length of the tin so that they appear in cross-section when the terrine is sliced.

7 Add the remaining half of the meat on top of the layer of gherkins and smooth it down. Fold over the edges of the bacon to enclose the meat in a neat parcel.

8 Preheat the oven to 150°C/300°F/Gas Mark 2. Place the terrine, in its tin, into a larger dish or roasting tray. Pour enough warm water in to reach most of the way up the sides of the tin, but not enough to risk drowning the terrine. Cover the terrine with a sheet of aluminium foil to stop it drying out and browning on top.

9 Bake the terrine in the preheaated oven for 1½ hours until it is cooked through. It can be checked with a probe thermometer: the internal temperature should reach at least 71°C/160°F. The terrine will release some fat during cooking and will shrink back from the edges of the tin. If you do not have a thermometer, a skewer can be used to test the centre, if less precisely.

10 Remove the terrine from the oven and when it is just cool enough to handle, turn it out from the tin onto a plate. Cover with foil and leave it in a cool place. Move it to the refrigerator once it has cooled to room temperature.

11 To serve, cut the terrine into slices approximately 1.5–2cm/½–¾in thick. Serve chilled as part of a cold meat platter. It can also be plated as a starter, served with a small salad of cherry tomatoes and rocket leaves perhaps, with an olive oil, honey and balsamic vinegar dressing.

ARDENNES-STYLE PÂTÉ

To adapt the pork shoulder terrine recipe into a delicious-tasting Ardennes-style coarse pâté terrine, some of the pork shoulder and belly can be replaced with pork liver. Use 400g/14oz pork liver, with 400g/14oz pork shoulder and 200g/7oz pork belly. Half of the meat and liver is puréed first, with the remaining half being broken down only slightly, leaving large chunks. Around 100g/3½oz of finely chopped bacon, smoked or unsmoked, can be added to the meat mixture to provide texture and flavour.

The terrine dish is lined with bacon or Parma ham as in the original recipe, and it is cooked for 1½ hours at 150°C/300°F/Gas mark 2 before being cooled. Once cold, serve in thick slices, along with some bread, perhaps a wholegrain loaf or crusty baguette.

HAGGIS

A real treat for any Burns Supper, or a versatile and economical ingredient to add interest and flavour to many other dishes, this haggis recipe is surprisingly easy to prepare and has all the classic rich, nutty and lightly-spiced flavours characteristic of the dish.

Every year, on the 25th of January, exiled Scots and their distant relatives around the world celebrate the work of the poet Robert Burns and the Scottish national dish. Haggis is traditionally served with 'bashed neeps and tatties' – swede (or rutabaga) and potato, boiled and mashed separately. One of my favourite Burns suppers was held many years ago in my flat, two floors up in a beautiful tenement building in Edinburgh's New Town. My friend Malcolm brought his bagpipes to pipe the haggis in. In the small dining room, the noise was incredible, and fortunately I had understanding neighbours.

Typically associated with Scotland, the exact origins of the dish are sometimes, controversially, disputed. The circumstances in which the dish evolved are lost in a haze of historical romance. What is known for certain is that haggis is a frugal peasant dish, intended to extract every last scrap of meat from the carcass of an animal. It makes use of the sheep's 'pluck' – the lungs, heart and liver. If you have any difficulty obtaining the whole pluck then it is sometimes easier to just get hold of the hearts.

Unlike salted prime cuts, offal dishes such as these would not tend to keep particularly well in the days before refrigeration. It is likely that these dishes were eaten around the time that the animal was slaughtered. Arguably the notion of celebration that surrounds this dish may have some origins in the 'giving of thanks' at that time, the family being assured of having meat on their plates for many months to come.

The dish makes use of the suet, the hard fat that lines the pluck organs. Unless you can obtain this from your butcher, use the shredded or frozen suet that can be bought for baking and pastry making. Suet has a slightly higher melting point compared to fats such as butter and a higher smoke point, which means that it can be heated to a higher temperature before the fat will begin to burn, and it is often used in traditional British cooking for both sweet and savoury dishes.

The oatmeal used here is the steel cut, pinhead or coarse variety rather than the finely ground or the rolled oats used to make porridge. The coarse grains will swell during cooking as they absorb water and the haggis will expand in size. For this reason, the casing should not be filled completely as it may burst. The oatmeal accounts for the plumpness of the haggis when it is served.

During the Burns Supper, the haggis is piped in and the meal is preceded by a recital of Burns' *Address to a Haggis*. During the reading, the haggis is cut open with a knife and, relieved of the pressure, the filling should take little encouragement to spill out from the casing, "*warm-reeking, rich*". Bagpipes, along with the *Address to the Haggis* and *The Selkirk Grace* are optional, however a dram of whisky is not.

INGREDIENTS

One lamb pluck, comprising lungs, heart and liver, weighing approximately 750g/1lb 10oz

Ox bung

2 medium onions

200g/7oz coarse oatmeal

200g/7oz shredded suet

15g/½oz salt

2.5ml/½ tsp ground white pepper

2.5ml/½ tsp dried thyme

2.5ml/½ tsp ground nutmeg

1.5ml/¼ tsp ground cinnamon

1.5ml/¼ tsp ground coriander

1 Wash the lamb pluck and place it into a saucepan with just enough cold water to cover it. Bring it to the boil and simmer over a low heat for an hour. The lungs will cause the pluck to float and they should be turned regularly or weighed down to ensure that they cook evenly. For such an unlikely set of ingredients, the aroma should already be rich and inviting while the pluck is cooking.

2 Remove the pan from the heat. Strain off the stock that has formed but reserve some of it to add back into the haggis filling later. Leave the meat for at least 30 minutes, until it is cool enough to handle. Meanwhile, soak the ox bung in cold water to soften.

3 Once the pluck meat has cooled, chop it into small rice-sized pieces using a sharp knife and place it in a mixing bowl. Finely chop the onions and add them to the chopped meat.

4 The oatmeal is gently browned to release its nutty flavour but should not be burnt. Toast it in a dry frying pan, stirring frequently to prevent it burning. If you take it too far, start again with fresh oatmeal rather than ruining the flavour of the haggis with the burnt oats. Add the oatmeal to the meat and onion.

5 Next add the suet with the salt, white pepper, thyme, nutmeg, cinnamon and coriander. Mix the ingredients together well and add just enough of the reserved stock to moisten the ingredients without making it sticky or 'claggy'.

6 Tie one end of the soaked ox bung using some butcher's string. The haggis can be filled using a sausage stuffer but the casing is quite wide in diameter and it is just as easy to use a spoon. It should be loosely rather than tightly filled, as the swelling oats can cause the haggis to burst during cooking. Tie the other end of the bung with string to seal in the filling, and prick a few small holes around the haggis with a pin or thin skewer to allow the juices and any trapped air to escape as it cooks.

7 Place the haggis into a pan of cold water, bring it to the boil and simmer it for 1½–2 hours, until the oatmeal swells and the haggis bulges. The haggis is served whole and sliced open at the table, allowing the filling to burst out onto the platter. Accompany the haggis with bashed neeps and tatties.

FAGGOTS

One of the traditional and neglected foods of England, this humble meatball makes use of some of the cheaper offal cuts but packs a rich and satisfying flavour and is surely due for a well-deserved revival.

Faggots are believed to have originated over 100 years ago, in Birmingham and the West Midlands of England; an area that is often described as the heart of the industrial revolution and at this time an economic powerhouse with a hard-working workforce. This thrifty dish would have been a cheap and satisfying meal, which made it highly popular with the working population and their families.

Today, in butchers' shops around England, it is still possible to find these small bundles of liver and chopped pork, mixed with breadcrumbs and wrapped in caul fat, the lacy membrane which surrounds the intestines of the sheep, pig or cow.

The faggot relies on the juices of the meat and offal being soaked up into the breadcrumbs to give maximum flavour for a minimum of meat, but it is the caul fat that is the secret to the texture of the dish. This thin membrane keeps the moisture inside the faggot, almost steaming it as it cooks, and the fat on the membrane melts in the oven adding to mouthfeel and flavour. Here, the recipe calls for pork shoulder and liver but other offal cuts such as heart have traditionally been added. The juices from the meat are locked into the breadcrumbs, so the faggots do not shrink much during cooking.

Caul fat is usually taken from pigs and is often packed by the pound weight (450g) which is almost certainly more than you will need for one meal, but the remainder can be frozen until needed. It keeps very well in the freezer and can be thawed in the refrigerator overnight ahead of time. If caul fat is not available, then the faggots can be wrapped in streaky bacon. It is, however, well worth sourcing this valuable ingredient to make the very best-quality faggots and the marbled appearance of the cooked caul adds something to the appeal of the dish.

Appropriately, this dish is flavoured with those herbs and spices that have a special place in English cookery – sage, pepper and nutmeg.

Faggots can be prepared in advance and refrigerated, before cooking, for a couple of days until needed. It is important to use the freshest shoulder and liver possible however; meat that is just on-date at the time that the faggots are made cannot be stored for this additional time. Old liver tastes unpleasant and it is well known that it spoils more easily than prime cuts of meat, often attributed to its higher levels of carbohydrate. The cooked faggots can also be refrigerated and reheated.

Faggots are traditionally served with mashed potatoes and a rich gravy. The mash should be buttered and very smooth – passing it through a sieve if necessary. A splash of milk can also be added. The gravy is prepared by sweating onions in some dripping until well-browned. Deglaze the pan with a splash of white wine then pour in a little veal, beef or chicken stock. If too thin, the gravy can be thickened with some cornflour, dissolved in a little cold water.

INGREDIENTS

Pork liver, weighing 400g/14oz

Pork shoulder with a generous amount of fat (or pork shoulder and belly), weighing 400g/14 oz

200ml/7fl oz milk

1 small onion

2 garlic cloves, chopped

100g/3½oz breadcrumbs, from stale white bread

1.5ml/¼ tsp salt

1.5ml/¼ tsp ground black pepper

1.5ml/¼ tsp dried thyme

1.5ml/¼ tsp ground nutmeg

1.5ml/¼ tsp dried sage

125g/4oz caul fat

1 The liver can be soaked in a little milk ahead of making the faggots. Soak it for up to 6 hours in the refrigerator and discard the milk afterwards.

2 Chop the pork shoulder and liver into rough cubes as this will make it easier to mince in the food processor. Chop the onion into small pieces.

3 Put the shoulder into the food processor and add the garlic. Pulse the power control a few times to begin breaking the meat into smaller pieces. Add the liver and 'blitz' it for up to 1 minute on full power. It should be roughly chopped rather than a smooth

paste – stop processing it once the desired texture is achieved.

4 The breadcrumbs can be made from stale white bread, pulverised in a food processor until they form a fine powder. I usually make up a bag of them in advance from the dry, but not mouldy, ends of loaves and freeze them until needed. Weigh out the breadcrumbs in a bowl and add the chopped meat and onion. Add the salt, pepper, thyme, nutmeg and sage to the mixture, stirring them in well to ensure that they are evenly distributed.

5 Unroll a length of the caul fat. Form the meat mixture into balls up to 5cm/2in in diameter. Place each ball in the centre of a piece of caul fat approximately twice as wide. Wrap up the caul to enclose each of the balls in a small parcel. The membrane should stick to itself easily. At this point, the faggots can be cooked immediately or refrigerated for up to 2 days until needed.

6 Preheat the oven to 180°C/350°F/Gas mark 4. Place the faggots on a greased baking tray. Do not overcrowd the tray but leave a small gap between them to prevent the faggots from sticking to each other. Place the baking tray in the oven and cook for 30 minutes, turning them once or twice during cooking.

7 Once the faggots are cooked through, they will have taken on a golden-brown colour. They do not usually shrink much during cooking. Serve them at once – traditionally they are accompanied by mashed potatoes and gravy.

BACON &
COOKED SAUSAGE

This chapter covers some of the ingredients in a classic
cooked breakfast, such as crispy bacon, juicy pork
sausages, and black and white puddings, but these foods
have a place in the kitchen that extends beyond the first
meal of the day.

For bacon, which is cured before cooking, different
salting techniques are covered, and some unusual
variations are introduced which are made with lamb
rather than pork. Pancetta and guanciale, which are
usually dried after curing, can also be found here.

In this chapter you will also find that other staple of
the butcher's counter, the sausage. A delicious range of
varieties are presented, each with its own distinctive
flavour. Most of these easy-to-follow recipes can be made
with ordinary kitchen equipment.

PORK SAUSAGES

Sausages are the ultimate comfort food and making your own could not be simpler.

Good-quality meat is the key to making a great sausage, which is perhaps ironic as they are often synonymous with poor-quality ingredients. Because the cooked sausage has been used historically as a way of using up scraps of meat that might be left over after butchery, there are a lot of commercial sausages which are of indifferent quality at best, or of dubious origin at worst.

Sausages are very easy to make but the effort involved in preparing and washing the equipment that is used to make them means that they are probably best made in larger batches. Once prepared, the sausages can be frozen until they are needed. If you happen to own a sausage mincer and stuffer, it is possible to turn out many sausages on the same run, as the basic recipe can be adapted to produce a wide variety of flavours. Careful preparation and a few hours work can reward the home charcutier with enough sausages to last for many meals over the following weeks. The ingredients are not particularly expensive, and it can be a cost-effective way to feel many hungry people.

The basic pork sausage recipe uses both shoulder and belly meat to achieve a good balance of lean and fat meat, with the fat providing flavour as well as contributing to the texture. To create the perfect sausage, aim to use around four times as much lean meat as fat, when selecting the cuts of meat. The shoulder meat will appear leaner than the belly, the latter having a more even proportion of fat and lean meat. Where less fat is used then the sausage will tend to dry out more during cooking.

There has been a tendency in pork production to selectively breed for leaner cuts of meat over the past few decades. As a result, the fat content of the meat has fallen considerably, and some traditional pig breeds have declined in number or have become extinct. Where the meat from one of the fattier breeds is used to make sausages, the proportion of the two meats could be adjusted, increasing the quantity of the leaner shoulder meat to around 800g/1lb 12oz for every 200g/7oz of belly pork.

The sausage mixture also needs a 'binder,' such as breadcrumbs or rusk, which helps to achieve a good texture by retaining moisture and preventing shrinkage during cooking. Breadcrumbs would have been used traditionally and it makes a great way of using up the ends of a stale (but not mouldy) loaf. Rusk is more commonly used now. This is a kind of dense breadcrumb, made without yeast, that has excellent moisture-binding properties. It is readily available from various suppliers but it is also possible to make your own rusk at home and a recipe has been provided here.

Salt is used to flavour the sausage mix rather than to cure the meat and the level is lower than is used in the salamis. 1.5–2% salt should suffice but it is possible to modify this according to personal preference. The salt will also bind some of the water, acting as a preservative. To check the level of salt in

the final product, fry a small patty of the sausage meat until thoroughly cooked and test the seasoning, adding a little more salt to the mix if necessary. It is better to add too little at first than too much as extra salt can always be added but it cannot be removed.

I have included descriptions of some of my favourite sausage recipes but once you're accustomed to the basic technique you will be able to experiment with different flavour ingredients to create your own unique sausages.

MAKING LINKS

1 To link sausages in twos, begin at the middle of a stuffed casing, and start by pinching the centre-point, gently twisting the casing.

2 Pinch the two ends at one sausage length and twist them together at the pinch point to create the loop.

3 Feed one of the ends through the previous loop to secure the link.

4 For longer lengths of sausage, this process is repeated until the end is reached. The two strands are pinched, twisted and one end is fed back through the resulting loop.

5 The sausages can alternatively be linked in threes. Form a single sausage near one end. Next form a loop, as shown in picture 2. The third sausage, running parallel to the loop, is formed by wrapping the longer end around the pinch point in the loop.

HOMEMADE RUSK

This is a simple recipe for rusk which can replace breadcrumbs when sausage-making.

900g/2lb plain/all-purpose or strong flour

10g/1½ tsp pure dried vacuum (PDV) salt

10ml/2 tsp sodium bicarbonate/baking soda

20ml/4 tsp potassium hydrogen tartrate/cream of tartar

200ml/7fl oz water

Sieve the flour, salt, baking soda and cream of tartar together. Add just enough of the water to make a smooth, but not sticky, dough. Knead it gently then roll out the dough to around 2cm/¾in thick and place it on a greased baking sheet.

Bake in the oven at 220°C/428°F/Gas mark 7 for 10–15 minutes. The top of the dough should be set. Slice the dough into fingers approximately 2cm/¾in wide, and turn them onto their sides on the baking tray. Reduce the heat and bake again at 190°C/374°F for 15–20 minutes until the dough is cooked through and has become dry and slightly brittle.

Stand the cooked dough on a wire rack until completely cool. Then, put the dough into a food processor and break it down to small crumbs. Store the rusk crumbs in a dry, airtight container until needed. As long as they are completely dry, they will keep for many months.

PLAIN PORK SAUSAGE

Pork shoulder, weighing 600g/1lb 3oz

Belly pork with a generous amount of fat, weighing 400g/14oz

50–100g/1¾–3½oz breadcrumbs or rusk

15–20g/½–¾oz pure dried vacuum (PDV) salt (amount according to taste)

7.5ml/1½ tsp finely ground black pepper

Natural hog casings

1 The casings are usually packed in salt to preserve them. Soak the casings in water for at least an hour before filling them.

2 Weigh the pork shoulder and belly. These should be chopped into evenly-sized chunks that are small enough to fit into the mincer. To make it easier to handle, firm the meat up by placing it in the freezer for up to 10 minutes before mincing it.

3 Mince the pork shoulder and belly through a 3–5mm/1/8–¼in plate into a small bowl. Alternate between mincing the shoulder and belly meat as this will make it easier to combine the two together.

4 Mix together well in a bowl. Weigh the breadcrumbs and mix into the meat mixture.

5 Add the PDV salt and the pepper, and mix them in well. Other seasoning ingredients would be added at this stage for different sausage flavours.

6 To fill the casings, you will need either a mechanical sausage stuffer or mincing machine with a filling nozzle. Alternatively, the casings may be filled manually using a large funnel, but this is a time-consuming task. Pack the sausage mixture into the filler.

7 Place a length of the hog casings over the end of the nozzle, making sure that the tip reaches the tied end of the casing. Do not try to tie off individual sausages at this stage; they will take their final shape during 'linking'. Crank the handle to begin filling, work slowly but steadily. The sausages should be evenly filled, with enough mixture to give the sausage a good shape. Do not overfill the sausages as they may burst when linking or cooking them.

8 Once filled, tie a knot on the end of the casing to contain the sausage mixture and trim off the excess casing. To link the sausages, gently pinch and twist the stuffed casing approximately half way along its length. Holding the casing at the pinch starts to form the shape of the sausage. Allow at least 10cm/4in per sausage. Pinch and twist the two strands of the stuffed casing to form a loop comprising two sausages. Feed one end of the casing through the loop to tie it off and continue linking the length of the casing until all the sausages are formed (see pages 154–155).

TO SERVE The sausages are raw and should be cooked throughout before eating. Grill or fry them before serving. Prick them to stop them exploding. They should be ready in about 10–12 minutes in the pan, slightly longer under the grill or broiler.

TOULOUSE SAUSAGE

This is a meaty and full-flavoured sausage, often used in cassoulet, a slow-cooked stew of meat and beans.

600g/1lb 3oz pork shoulder

400g/14oz belly pork with a generous amount of fat

200ml/6¾fl oz red wine

15–20g/½–¾oz pure dried vacuum (PDV) salt (amount according to taste)

10ml/2 tsp finely ground black pepper

5ml/1 tsp minced or crushed garlic

50g/1¾ breadcrumbs or rusk

Natural hog casings

The pork shoulder and belly should be marinated in the red wine for several hours before mincing. Keep the pork and wine mixture in the refrigerator, for 6–18 hours, in a covered, non-metallic bowl. Discard the wine.

Mince the meat as for the plain pork sausage recipe, and mix in the PDV salt, pepper, garlic and breadcrumbs, before filling the mixture into the natural casings.

CUMBERLAND SAUSAGE

A distinctive coiled sausage which originates from the north-west of England.

600g/1lb 3oz pork shoulder

400g/14oz belly pork with a generous amount of fat

15–20g/½–¾oz pure dried vacuum (PDV) salt (amount according to taste)

5ml/1 tsp finely ground black pepper

5ml/1 tsp finely ground white pepper

50–100g/1¾–3½oz breadcrumbs or rusk

Natural hog casings

Mince the meat as for the plain pork sausage recipe, and add in the PDV salt, black and white pepper and breadcrumbs before filling the mixture into the natural casings. Instead of linking the sausages in small 10cm/4in lengths, allow around 30–40cm/12–16in per sausage.

LINCOLNSHIRE SAUSAGE

Like chine (page 114), this Lincolnshire sausage is dominated by herby flavours.

600g/1lb 3oz pork shoulder

400g/14oz belly pork with a generous amount of fat

15–20g/½–¾oz pure dried vacuum (PDV) salt (according to taste)

5ml/1 tsp finely ground black pepper

10–15ml/2–3 tsp finely chopped fresh sage

50–100g/1¾–3½oz breadcrumbs or rusk

Natural hog casings

Remove woody stalks and chop the sage leaves finely to provide around 2–3 tsp of the chopped herb. Mince the meat as for the plain pork sausage recipe, and add in the PDV salt, black pepper, chopped sage and breadcrumbs, before filling the mixture into the natural casings. Instead of linking the sausages in small 10cm/4in lengths, allow around 30–40cm/12–16in per sausage.

° WILTSHIRE SAUSAGE

A meaty sausage from the south-west of England, with warm flavours of mace, nutmeg and ginger.

600g/1lb 3oz pork shoulder

400g/14oz belly pork with a generous amount of fat

15–20g/½–¾oz pure dried vacuum (PDV) salt (amount according to taste)

5ml/1 tsp finely ground black pepper

5ml/1 tsp ground mace

2.5ml/½ tsp ground ginger

2.5ml/½ tsp ground nutmeg

50–100g/1¾–3½oz breadcrumbs or rusk

Natural hog casings

Mince the meat as for the plain pork sausage recipe, and add in the PDV salt, black pepper, mace, ginger, nutmeg and breadcrumbs before filling the mixture into the natural casings. Link the sausages into 10cm/4in lengths.

STILTON AND APPLE SAUSAGE

An interesting flavoured sausage which marries the flavours of salty Stilton with sweet apple. Large chunks of apple hold a lot of water and can sometimes burst the sausage, so here the fruit is grated rather than chopped.

600g/1lb 3oz pork shoulder

400g/14oz belly pork with a generous amount of fat

15–20g/½–¾oz pure dried vacuum (PDV) salt (amount according to taste)

5ml/1 tsp finely ground black pepper

100g/3½oz Stilton cheese, broken into fine crumbs

1 apple, peeled and grated

100g/3½oz breadcrumbs or rusk

Natural hog casings

Mince the meat as for the plain pork sausage recipe. Add in the PDV salt, black pepper, Stilton cheese, grated apple and breadcrumbs, and mix together very well before filling the mixture into the natural casings. Link the sausages into 10cm/4in lengths.

OXFORD SAUSAGE

A traditional sausage variety from the south of England, flavoured with mace and sage.

300g/10½oz pork shoulder

300g/10½oz pork belly

400g/14oz veal

15–20g/½–¾oz pure dried vacuum (PDV) salt (amount according to taste)

5ml/1 tsp finely ground black pepper

5ml/1 tsp ground mace or nutmeg

5ml/1 tsp chopped fresh sage

100g/3½oz breadcrumbs or rusk

Natural hog casings

Remove any woody stalks and finely chop the sage, to provide around 1 tsp of chopped herb. Mince the meat as for the plain pork sausage recipe, and add in the PDV salt, black pepper, mace or nutmeg, sage and breadcrumbs, before filling the mixture into the natural casings. Link the sausages into 10cm/4in lengths.

BOEREWORS

A meaty, highly spiced sausage which originates in South Africa. The perfect addition to any braai or barbecue. This sausage contains no rusk or breadcrumbs.

600g/1lb 3oz beef brisket

300g/10½oz lamb shoulder

200g/7oz pork shoulder

100g/3½oz pork belly

15–20g/½–¾oz pure dried vacuum (PDV) salt (amount according to taste)

15ml/3 tbsp wine vinegar or cider vinegar

5ml/1 tsp ground coriander

5ml/1 tsp ground nutmeg

1.5ml/¼ tsp ground allspice

1.5ml/¼ tsp ground cloves

Natural sheep or hog casings

Mince the beef brisket, lamb shoulder, pork shoulder and belly as for the plain sausage recipe. Add in the PDV salt, vinegar, coriander, nutmeg, allspice and cloves, and mix well. Fill the mixture into the natural casings and link the sausages into 15cm/6in lengths.

MERGUEZ

A classic North African lamb sausage, which makes an excellent addition to couscous and tagine dishes. The recipe requires good-quality harissa, which is a delicious and hot chilli paste from the Maghreb regions of Tunisia, Morocco, Algeria and Libya. Sheep casings can be more delicate than hog casings so take care to avoid overfilling them.

900g/2lb lamb shoulder

300g/10½oz lamb or beef fat or suet

15–20g/½–¾oz pure dried vacuum (PDV) salt (amount according to taste)

5ml/1 tsp finely ground sweet paprika

5ml/1 tsp harissa paste

5ml/1 tsp ground cumin

2 garlic cloves, crushed

50g/1¾oz breadcrumbs or rusk

Natural sheep casings

Mince the lamb shoulder as for the plain pork sausage recipe. Add in the suet (or minced fat), PDV salt, paprika, harissa, cumin, garlic and breadcrumbs before filling the mixture into the sheep casings. Link the sausages into 10–15cm/4–6in lengths.

BLACK PUDDING & WHITE PUDDING

Do not be confused by the name 'pudding' – these are not sweet treats, but frugal savoury dishes, rich in iron, originating in the thriftiest tradition of European peasant cooking. They are nonetheless a delightful addition to any fried breakfast. The precious ingredients of fat, with or without blood, are adsorbed into oatmeal to make a delicious and substantial meal. In the days before refrigeration it is said that the puddings were stored under oatmeal to preserve them.

Growing up in the north of England, I was quickly introduced to white pudding and the not dissimilar black or 'blood' pudding, made from some of the leftover bits of pig which did not typically lend themselves to curing and aging. There are similar blood pudding dishes to be found across Europe, from the famous boudin noir and boudin blanc of France, to the morcilla of Spain, and Polish kaszanka, made from blood and offal. In the British Isles there are numerous regional variations of the puddings, such as the Stornoway black pudding from the Western Isles of Scotland, highly seasoned but not spicy; the Bury black pudding from Lancashire, studded with pristine white fat; and the famed Clonakilty black pudding, from County Cork in the Republic of Ireland, which is still made to a secret recipe dating back to 1880.

To make the black pudding, you usually need access to fresh blood which is not always readily available unless you are slaughtering your own animals. This is a messy business and the blood, once dried, can be hard to wash off. A dash of brandy was often added to the blood to prevent it from clotting. Dried blood is available from some sausage-making suppliers and this can be used as an alternative; the dried blood should be rehydrated in a little warm water before use.

To serve, cut generous slices of the black or white pudding, fry or grill them on either side until lightly browned, and serve immediately. They are excellent served as part of a breakfast fry-up but also make an interesting addition to white bean casseroles and warm salads.

BLACK PUDDING

Fresh pig's blood, 250ml/9fl oz

Pork fat, weighing 250g/9oz

2 white onions

200g/7oz coarse or pinhead oatmeal

10ml/2 tsp pure dried vacuum (PDV) salt

10ml/2 tsp ground black pepper

5ml/1 tsp ground mace

2.5ml/½ tsp ground cinnamon

100g/3¾oz shredded beef suet

Natural hog casings

1 While you make the sausage, soak the natural casings in a bowl of water for 2 hours to soften them before filling them.

2 Sieve the pig's blood into a bowl or jug, to remove any of the dark red clots. This can be a nasty job as the jelly-like clots are rather offputting but don't let it deter you from the recipe!

3 Chop the pork fat into small cubes. Peel and cut the onions into small pieces.

4 Add the fat, along with the chopped onion, to a frying pan over a medium-low heat and allow them to brown slightly. The fat will sweat slightly.

5 Place the oatmeal in a large mixing bowl, and add the sweated fat and the fried onions to the oatmeal. Next add the PDV salt, pepper, mace and cinnamon, add the suet and mix all the ingredients together well.

6 Then, pour in enough of the sieved blood to make a sticky paste.

7 To fill the casings, you will need either a mechanical sausage stuffer or mincing machine with a filling nozzle. The puddings should only be loosely filled, and they may look a little untidy, or even unattractively saggy, before cooking. The oatmeal will expand during cooking and an overfilled pudding may burst during cooking.

8 Bring a large pan of water to the boil and turn down the heat to a gentle simmer. Prick the casing of the puddings in one or two places and lower the

puddings into the hot water. It will take about 30 minutes to 1 hour to cook, by which time the oatmeal will have softened and the pudding mixture will have swollen to fill the casing.

9 Remove the puddings from the pan and leave them to cool. Once they have done so, they should be stored in the refrigerator, for up to a week, until needed.

WHITE PUDDING

Pork fat, weighing 250g/9oz

2 white onions

200g/7oz coarse or pinhead oatmeal

10ml/2 tsp pure dried vacuum (PDV) salt

10ml/2 tsp ground black pepper

5ml/1 tsp ground mace

2.5ml/½ tsp ground cinnamon

100g/3¾oz shredded beef suet

About 250ml/8fl oz water

Natural hog casings

1 While you make the puddings, soak the natural casings in a bowl of water for 2 hours to soften before filling them.

2 Chop the pork fat into small cubes. Peel and cut the onions into small pieces.

3 Add the fat along with the chopped onion to a frying pan over a medium-low heat and allow them to brown slightly. The fat will sweat slightly.

4 Place the oatmeal in a large mixing bowl, and add the sweated fat and the fried onions to the oatmeal. Next add the salt, pepper, mace and cinnamon, add the suet, and mix all the ingredients together well. Then, pour in just enough of the water to make a sticky paste.

5 To fill the casings, you will need either a mechanical sausage stuffer or mincing machine with a filling nozzle. Alternatively, the casings may be filled manually using a large funnel, but this is more time-consuming. The puddings should only be loosely filled, and they may look a little untidy, or even unattractively saggy, before cooking. The oatmeal will expand during cooking and an overfilled pudding may burst during cooking.

6 Bring a large pan of water to the boil and turn down the heat to a gentle simmer. Prick the casing of the puddings in one or two places and lower the puddings into the hot water. It will take about 30 minutes to 1 hour to cook, by which time the oatmeal will have softened and the pudding mixture will have swollen to fill the casing.

7 Remove from the pan and leave them to cool. Once they have cooled, they should be stored in the refrigerator, for up to a week, until needed.

DRY-CURED BACON

Making your own bacon is so easy, and the flavour is so infinitely superior to that of shop-bought bacon, that you may not ever want to go back. Once you have mastered the basic recipe, you can experiment with various combinations of ingredients in the cure to produce your own unique bacon.

My earliest food memory is of the smell and sound of bacon frying over breakfast with my grandparents. You have to spend quite a lot of money these days to buy bacon that is as delicious as it was all those years ago. Like freshly brewed coffee or the smell of bread in the oven, there is something wonderfully inviting about the aroma of bacon as it is frying, though it is a pity that so much bacon these days has such a disappointing flavour.

The bacon curing process is very straightforward, and involves nothing more complicated than packing a cut of pork in salt and a combination of spices. The resulting bacon is dried slightly for about one day. It can be sliced and grilled, broiled or fried, but can be kept almost indefinitely by drying it further as is done in the case of pancetta.

There is a marked difference in the moisture content of traditionally cured bacon as opposed to the slices of bacon typically available in your local supermarket. These are high in moisture and would spoil if kept for longer than the use-by date specified. This is likely to be a symptom of modern curing methods which leave more moisture in the bacon, the cause of the white foam that fizzes and pops when frying before starting to catch and burn on the pan.

The cuts of meat usually used to make bacon are pork belly, which produces the type of bacon referred to as 'streaky' in the UK and sometimes 'side pork' in the USA, or back bacon which is a cut consisting of the lean pork loin and small amount of the fatty belly at the thin end of each rasher (or thin slice). The process for either cut of pork is the same but belly pork is likely to be easier to get hold of and, thanks to the marbling of fat, much more flavoursome. Cut the curing time by about one day if you are using pork loin rather than belly.

While home-made bacon is delicious even when served as simply as being placed between slices of fresh bread with a little ketchup, I use it to make one of my favourite simple suppers: fry cubed bacon with some onions gently in a pan until the onions are soft and the bacon is lightly browned on the edges. Add some shredded savoy cabbage which has been soaked in a pan of freshly boiled water for a few minutes and enough double or heavy cream to cover the base of the pan. Stir it over the heat for a few minutes until the cream begins to thicken, and serve immediately with boiled or roasted potatoes.

Both dry-cured and brined bacon can also be smoked after salting. For more information on cold-smoking techniques, see the instructions on pages 225–226.

INGREDIENTS

**One pork belly, weighing approximately
1–1.5kg/2lb 2oz–3lb 3oz**

100g/3½oz pure dried vacuum (PDV) salt

20g/¾oz golden or soft brown sugar

5ml/1 tsp crushed black pepper

2.5ml/½ tsp ground nutmeg

**Curing Salt #1, 2.5g/¹⁄₁₆oz per 1 kg/2.2lb of meat,
optional (see the notes on curing salts on pages
16–19 and always follow the manufacturer's
instructions)**

1 Weigh out the PDV salt, sugar, pepper and nutmeg, adjusting the quantities for the exact weight of the pork belly. (This can be adjusted by dividing the weight of your meat by that stated in the recipe, and then multiplying each ingredient by the result.) Mix these ingredients together well. Add the curing salt if using, and mix in very thoroughly.

2 Rinse the pork belly and pat it dry with a kitchen towel. Place it into a plastic food bag or lidded tub. Coat it with the cure mixture, ensuring that it is covered evenly on all sides. Cover, or if using a plastic bag, clip or tie securely as the cure will draw water out from the pork to create a small quantity of brine.

3 The pork belly should be kept in the refrigerator at a temperature of 3–5°C/37–41°F and left to cure for 5 days. Redistribute the cure over the surface of the meat each day. This can usually be done quite easily by shaking the bag or tub, so not an onerous task.

4 Once the meat has cured, remove the bacon from the bag or tub and wash off any excess cure. It should look darker at this point and will feel firmer as much of the moisture has been lost from the meat. Leave it to soak in fresh water for 30–60 minutes then drain it and pat the bacon dry with a paper towel.

5 The bacon should be hung on a bacon comb to dry slightly in a cool, dark place for 24 hours, which will allow the outside of the bacon to form a slightly shiny protective coat.

TO SERVE When you are ready to serve it, slice the bacon finely into rashers using a sharp knife. For best results, only slice as much as you need each time, as the bacon will keep best this way. If you have to slice it all, wrap the slices in some clingfilm or food wrap, keep them in the refrigerator and use them up within 5 days. Alternatively, divide up the rashers and freeze them in small parcels for use over the coming month.

If you are making or cutting a lot of bacon then it might be more efficient to use a light-duty meat slicer. Be careful to wash the slicer carefully before and after using it to cut ready-to-eat charcuterie products (i.e. those which do not require cooking as they are already cooked or dried after curing).

VARIATIONS

Once you have mastered the bacon curing process, it is possible to experiment with other flavour combinations in the cure. Here are some suggestions, but there are many others for you to discover yourself. To smoke your bacon, see the instructions on pages 225–226 for more details.

Treacle-cured bacon Replace the soft brown sugar with 15ml/1 tbsp of thick black treacle or molasses, for a more intense flavour. All the other ingredients are added in the same quantity as in the main recipe. You will find the treacle is harder to apply than the sugar – smear it on as evenly as possible at first, then once some water has been drawn out of the pork belly, it should thin the treacle. This will make it easier to redistribute the cure over the pork in the subsequent days.

Once it is ready, after 5 days curing, scrape off any excess cure and rinse the bacon, then soak it for 1 hour in fresh water before patting it dry with some kitchen towel. Dry the bacon for 24 hours and store as stated in the main recipe.

Maple-cured bacon Maple syrup is more a more expensive option than sugar or treacle, but the flavour is quite incredible. Replace the sugar with 15ml/1 tbsp of maple syrup. The syrup is slightly easier to apply than treacle.

After curing for 5 days, rinse the excess cure from the bacon, soak it for an hour and pat it dry with kitchen towel. Dry the bacon for 24 hours and store as stated in the main recipe.

Bourbon-, marmalade- and chipotle-cured bacon This sticky glaze makes an incredible, intensely flavoured bacon with a little heat and smokiness coming from the chipotles, which are dried smoked jalapeño chillies. The cure should be made by mixing the salt, sugar and spices with 15ml/1 tbsp marmalade, 15ml/1 tbsp bourbon whiskey, and 1.5ml/¼ tsp finely chopped or flaked chipotle chillies (a little goes a long way!).

The cure should be left on for 5 days. Rinse the excess cure from the pork belly, soak it in fresh water for 1 hour and pat it dry with kitchen towel at the end of this time. Dry the bacon for 24 hours and store as stated in the main recipe.

Five spice-cured bacon Another sticky glaze, this time with Chinese-inspired flavours. The cure should be made by omitting the nutmeg but mixing the salt, sugar and black pepper with 15ml/1 tbsp dark soy sauce and 1.5–2.5ml/¼–½ tsp Chinese five spice. The cure should be left on for 5 days. After this time, rinse the excess cure from the pork belly, soak it in fresh water for 1 hour and pat it dry with kitchen towel at the end of this time. Dry the bacon for 24 hours and store as stated in the main recipe.

Honey- and mustard-cured bacon To prepare this cure, mix the salt, nutmeg and black pepper. Omit the sugar but instead add 30ml/2 tbsp of clear honey and 15ml/1 tbsp of wholegrain mustard. Smear the mixture liberally over the pork and leave it in the refrigerator to cure for 5 days. When it is ready, rinse off any excess cure and pat the pork belly dry using a kitchen towel. Dry the bacon for 24 hours and store as stated in the main recipe.

BRINE-CURED BACON

Brine-curing is a rapid way to salt pork and makes deliciously moist bacon in a much shorter time than dry-curing.

The realisation that brining was an effective way of salting meat products possibly came about by accident rather than design. A quantity of brine forms around meat when it is dry-cured with salt. When large quantities of meat are dry-salted together, it forms a large quantity of brine in the salting tub. Salt was a valuable ingredient in the days before refrigeration, far too expensive to discard even when the salt barrel became damp, or even wet. It would not have taken long to establish that foods which were cured in the resulting brine were preserved just as effectively as those which were dry-salted.

Perhaps the best-known of the brine cures, the Wiltshire cure, originates from the county of the same name, located in the south-west of England and historically a centre for pig farming. Today the Wiltshire cure is used for a variety of ham and bacon products. It is typically a 'live cure' which means that it contains microorganisms which contribute to flavour development in the bacon. These are typically species of *Micrococcus* and *Lactobacillus* similar to those used to ferment salami and which may be present at levels exceeding 1,000,000 per millilitre (0.03 fluid ounce). These bacterial populations can grow naturally over time or may be introduced deliberately through the use of a small quantity of starter culture.

Once a brine is made, which may involve the deliberate addition of a starter culture to inoculate the brine, it might not be changed for a considerable period of time, possibly many years. It will, however, be monitored for concentration of salt and curing salts (nitrate and nitrite) as well as pH (a measure of acidity). The pH of the brine is typically 5.0–6.9 and should remain stable, as should the temperature. Fluctuations in these parameters may indicate a loss of process control and increased potential for growth of spoilage bacteria or pathogens. The brine should be regularly stirred up in order to aerate it. The brine can change colour over time as a result of some of the meat juices, but as long as the salt and pH of the brine are controlled, any solids are filtered out and the tank is topped up with some fresh brine periodically, the growth of harmful microorganisms will be prevented.

Brines can be an important part of the flavour development of cured meat products. The exact composition of a commercial brine may vary from one processor to another, but the principle remains the same. The home charcutier might find that as their brine microflora develops, its unique microbial balance brings out increasingly complex flavours in the meat. However, without the ability to monitor brine pH and composition, the maintenance of the brine tank over an extended period of time may prove to be very difficult. It is important that the salt is replenished adequately and that nitrite neither increases to toxic levels nor falls in such a way that might compromise safety. If this is not practically possible then it might be best to make a fresh brine every time.

The brine is applied under strict temperature control to maintain the freshness of the meat. Pork is immersed in the brine for a period of one or more days at 2–5°C/35–41°F before 'maturation' at the same temperature for a similar period. Smaller cuts of pork, weighing one or two kilos (or two to four pounds), can be brined effectively without a brine pump, but the recipe may not work as well with smaller or larger cuts of meat. It depends on the cut of meat but I would work on the basis of at least an equal volume of meat to brine.

INGREDIENTS

Belly or back pork, weighing around 1–1.5kg/ 2lb 2oz–3lb 3oz

Brine made of 340g/12 oz salt for every 3.78ltr/6.7pints/1 US gallon cold water

Curing Salt #1, 2.5g/¹⁄₁₆ oz per 1 kg/2.2lb of meat, optional (see the notes on pages 16–19 and always follow the manufacturer's instructions)

0.5g bioprotective starter culture such as Christian Hansen F-LC SafePro, containing *Staphylococcus xylosus* and lactic acid bacteria dissolved in the brine, optional

45ml/3 tbsp brown sugar

3–4 bay leaves

5–10 juniper berries

15ml/1 tbsp black peppercorns

1 Make up the brine in a container such as a food-grade plastic tub that is large enough to hold the brine as well as the meat, and which will fit in a refrigerator. The tub should be cleaned before used.

2 To the measured water, add the brining salt, the curing salt if using, and the starter if using. Add the sugar, bay leaves, juniper berries and peppercorns to the brine, stir well and keep it in the refrigerator. It can be used immediately, though for best results make it up a day or so before it is needed, to allow the flavours to infuse into the brine.

3 Trim off any loose scraps of meat to give a neat, even shape. Rinse the meat and place it into the tub of brine.

4 Keep the brining meat in the refrigerator, maintaining the temperature at 3–5°C/37–41°F for the duration of the brining time. This should be around 1–2 days per kg/2lb 2oz of meat. Turn the meat in the brine several times during brining to avoid leaving parts of the meat exposed to the air. This will ensure that the salt is adsorbed as evenly as possible on all sides.

5 After 1–2 days, remove the meat from the brine. (If you are keeping the brine, top up the salt and sieve out the herbs.) The pork may feel firmer and may have darkened slightly. Rinse the pork and place it into a bowl or pan of clean cold water, large enough to fit it completely. Soak the pork in the water for at least 15 minutes.

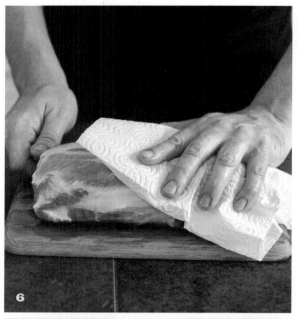

6 Remove the pork from the water, and pat it dry with kitchen paper.

7 Place the pork on two or three butcher's hooks, or a bacon comb, and hang it to dry in a cool, dark place (around 5–10°C/41–50°F) for 1–2 days to allow the rind to form. The outside of the bacon should dry slightly, with the rind taking on a glossy appearance, during this time.

8 The bacon, once ready, can be stored in a refrigerator below 8°C/46°F until needed. Use it up within 2–3 weeks or slice and freeze the rashers of bacon in small portions, which can be thawed easily a few hours before they are needed. Thaw frozen bacon thoroughly in the refrigerator prior to cooking and serving it.

9 Once the bacon has cured, it should be sliced finely into rashers, using a meat slicer or a sharp cook's knife. To avoid the risk of cross contamination, always wash the meat slicer thoroughly after it has been used to cut raw charcuterie products, and before cutting ready-to-eat cured products.

TO SERVE The bacon must be cooked before serving it. The bacon should be fried or grilled for a few minutes on each side until cooked through. Bacon can also be cold-smoked after curing – see the chapter on smoking on pages 225–226.

GUANCIALE

Cured pig cheeks create a form of bacon that has an incredible intensity of flavour, and a rich marbling of delicious fat that brings depth and complexity. It is typically used as fine shreds to liven up a pasta sauce.

Guanciale, which takes its name from the Italian word for 'cheek' (*guancia*) but which directly translates as 'pillow', is a delightful charcuterie product. It is one which is very rarely seen in the shops, however, possibly a victim of the fashion towards leaner meat, often at the expense of flavour.

Guanciale is commonly associated with the Italian region of Lazio, which is an important agricultural centre surrounding Rome and specifically with the town of Amatrice. Guanciale is one of the key ingredients of the slightly spicy sugo all'amatriciana, along with tomatoes and pecorino, a hard sheep's milk cheese. To be truly authentic, bucatini is the pasta of choice to serve with sliced guanciale, as pictured here, along with grated pecorino.

The cheeks shown in this recipe have had a lot of fat trimmed away. Guanciale can be cured from cheeks which still have a good amount of fat on them; absolutely delicious but richer and heavier.

AMATRICIANA SAUCE

To prepare amatriciana sauce, fry some sliced guanciale in a pan over a low heat with a little olive oil. Allow for enough guanciale to make up approximately one quarter of the weight of pasta served with it. Add one onion and a deseeded chilli, both finely chopped. The fat of the bacon will start to become transparent as it cooks, while the onion will soften and start to caramelise. When this happens, pour in a little white wine to deglaze the pan and stir for a minute while it bubbles up. Add some ripe tomatoes, peeled and chopped with the hard parts cut out. Cook over a low heat for 20 minutes while the tomato breaks down and the sauce thickens. Season and serve at once with cooked bucatini or other pasta and plenty of finely grated pecorino cheese.

INGREDIENTS

Pork cheeks, weighing approximately 500g/1lb 1oz

27g/1 oz pure dried vacuum (PDV) salt

14g/½oz golden or brown sugar

2.5ml/½ tsp dried thyme

2.5ml/½ tsp crushed black pepper

2.5ml/½ tsp fennel seeds

1–2 dried juniper berries

1 Weigh the pork cheeks and record the weight. You may need this to calculate the weight loss of the meat after drying.

2 Weigh out the PDV salt and sugar, adjusting their quantities according to the weight of the pork cheek. Add the thyme, black pepper and fennel seeds. Crush the juniper berries in a pestle and mortar and add them too. Mix the cure ingredients together well.

3 Rinse the pork cheeks and pat dry with a kitchen towel. Place the cheeks into a plastic food bag and pour in the cure ingredients, making sure that the meat is covered evenly on all sides. Clip or tie the top of the plastic bag securely to seal it; the cure may draw a small amount of water out of the pig cheeks to form a brine.

4 The pork cheek should be kept in the refrigerator at a temperature of 3–5°C/37–41°F while it cures. Leave it for 7 days, redistributing the cure over the surface of the meat every day or two by shaking and massaging the bag.

5 Once the meat has cured, remove the guanciale from the bag and wash off any excess cure. The meat may look darker at this point and can feel slightly firmer. Leave the guanciale to soak in fresh water for 10 minutes before draining it and patting it dry with a paper towel.

6 Place the guanciale on butcher's hooks and hang to dry in a cool, dark place (around 10–12°C/50–54°F) for at least 7 days. It will continue to lose moisture and become firmer if hung for longer, possibly for up to 2 months, and will become more intensely flavoured, if a little too salty. While it isn't often seen on the charcuterie platter, should you want to serve the guanciale without cooking it, you will need to leave it to dry until it loses 30% of its initial weight.

TO SERVE When you are ready to serve it, slice the guanciale finely into rashers using a sharp knife or a meat slicer. Only slice as much as you need each time and use some clingfilm or food wrap to protect the cut face of the meat from drying out when storing it, wrapped in some greaseproof paper. Guanciale is best when fried like bacon, the fat giving it a rich and luxurious mouthfeel.

PANCETTA

A variation of the bacon recipe, pancetta owes much of its flavour to the highly aromatic cure which is used to prepare it. It makes a versatile addition to almost any savoury dish from spaghetti carbonara to macaroni cheese.

Once the preserve of the specialist delicatessen, pancetta has started to appear in the supermarkets. It can usually be found in the aisle with the bacon, labelled as 'needs to be cooked'. There can be little to tell the two apart, visually, which is unfortunate because good pancetta is a remarkable product that lends itself to a variety of dishes.

In its native Italy, pancetta can be found in two forms: a flat slab or *stesa*, and *arrotolata*, which is rolled up tightly and sliced on the round face. The curing process is the same for both varieties, the only difference being that the *arrotolata* pancetta is rolled up tightly and tied into shape using butcher's string before it is dried. The flat *stesa* pancetta is dried without rolling and takes the shape of the pork belly from which it was made.

The salt and sugar should be weighed carefully for this recipe, however the quantities of the herbs and spices may be adjusted according to personal taste and it is even possible to substitute other herbs or spices instead, such as fennel or paprika. The latter is sometimes used to make an eastern European cured pork product called *salo*. While this is typically made with back fat, like the Lardo on pages 50–53, it is possible to use pork belly instead and cure it following the pancetta recipe described here,

removing the juniper berries and thyme but replacing them instead with a couple of tablespoons of Hungarian hot paprika.

INGREDIENTS
Pork belly, weighing approximately 1kg/2lb 2oz
35g/1¼oz pure dried vacuum (PDV) salt
10g/1½ tsp golden or brown sugar
4–5 dried juniper berries
5ml/1 tsp ground nutmeg
10ml/2 tsp dried thyme
5ml/1 tsp garlic powder
10ml/2 tsp coarse ground black pepper
2 bay leaves

Curing Salt, 2.5g/¹⁄₁₆ oz per 1 kg/2.2lb of meat, optional (see the notes on pages 16–19 and always follow the manufacturer's instructions); use Curing Salt #2 if drying the pancetta or Curing Salt #1 if cooking it

1 Rinse the pork belly and pat it dry with a paper kitchen towel. The skin can either be left on, or removed to make the pancetta easier to cut, but the bones must be removed.

2 Slice away the ribs if still attached or ask your butcher to do this for you.

3 If still attached, carve the skin off neatly by sliding the knife in just underneath the skin and slowly separating it from the fat underneath, peeling it back.

4 Weigh the pork and record the weight. This will be essential for calculating the quantities of cure, and also to calculate moisture loss during drying.

5 To prepare the cure, adjusting the quantities for the exact weight of the pork belly, weigh out the PDV salt and sugar. Crush the juniper berries using a pestle and mortar and add to the salt and sugar along with the nutmeg, thyme, garlic powder, and pepper. Mix it all together well, adding the bay leaves.

6 If using the curing salt, follow the supplier's instructions with regard to the quantity, and mix in very thoroughly so it is evenly distributed throughout the cure.

7 Rub the cure mixture over the pork belly to evenly distribute it on both sides.

8 Put the pork belly into the plastic food bag or butcher's bag and again make sure that the pork belly is evenly coated with the cure mixture on all sides. Clip or tie the top of the plastic bag to seal it. The bag should be kept in the refrigerator at a temperature of 3–5°C/37–41°F and left to cure for 10–14 days. Redistribute the cure over the surface of the meat every day or two. This can usually be done quite easily by shaking and massaging the bag.

9 Once the pancetta has been cured, remove it from the bag and brush off any excess cure. It should appear darker and feel firmer by this point as much of the moisture has been lost from the meat.

10 Leave the pancetta to soak in fresh water for 5 minutes then drain it and pat it dry with a paper towel. It can be cooked like bacon at this point but, for best results, it should be dried.

11 If making the rolled pancetta, place it flat on a table, the lean meat uppermost, and begin to roll the short end in towards the centre. Roll it as tightly as possible to avoid leaving large gaps in the middle which could start to go mouldy.

12 The rolled pancetta can be secured with a skewer while it is tied as it can be tricky otherwise without some helping hands. Use the butcher's knot to secure the roll, tying it in a couple of places (see the tip box).

13 To dry it, the pancetta should be hung on a bacon comb or butcher's hook in a cool, dark place such as a meat safe or larder at 10–12°C/50–54°F. Make sure that pests such as flying insects are excluded – the pancetta can be loosely covered in muslin if necessary. Besides the risk that they might transmit food-borne illnesses, there are few things as disappointing, and revolting, as finding your cured meat wriggling with maggots. Leave it to dry until it has lost at least 35% of its initial weight. This may take a month or more depending on the relative humidity and size of the cut of meat. The pancetta may drip slightly in the early part of the drying period.

TO SERVE When it is ready, the pancetta can be sliced using a sharp knife or meat slicer. It may be served without cooking and makes a great addition to a charcuterie platter if sliced finely. It can also be used as an ingredient, however, its intensity of flavour adding depth to various cooked dishes.

When slicing the pancetta, only cut as much as you need each time and wrap the cut face in some clingfilm or food wrap to prevent it from drying out. It will keep quite well over the following months if it is wrapped in some greaseproof paper and stored in the refrigerator.

THE BUTCHER'S KNOT

Lie the joint of meat on a length of butcher's string. Bring the short upper end over the meat. Loop this short end around the longer end, passing behind it on the right and coming back out on the left. Pass the short end through the loop that has been formed to make a simple overhand knot. Pull it tight to secure the joint of meat.

To prevent the overhand knot from slipping, fold a loop in the long end of the string. Take a bight (U-shaped looped section) of the string in your left hand and twist it 180 degrees in an anti-clockwise direction. Pass the short end down through the loop and pull both ends to tighten the knot. Trim off the ends.

LAMB & MUTTON BACON

This unusual bacon recipe makes use of the complex yet delicate flavours of the breast cut of a lamb. If you can find it, use mutton instead for a stronger, more 'gamey' flavour.

It should perhaps come as no surprise that, in the days before the ready availability of the refrigerator many other types of meat were preserved by salting them. In his diary, George Orwell, the author of 1984 and Animal Farm, recorded the recipe for 'macon'. This was a type of bacon made in Scotland, using a leg or shoulder of mutton. It was cured in salt, sugar and saltpetre (potassium nitrate) for a week before being smoked over sawdust, wood or peat, but never pine or coal. The macon would be smoked for up to a week, the wood dampened with an occasional sprinkle of water, and kept smouldering by a reheating a flat-iron each day and burying it in sawdust.

Today there are a growing number of farms, butchers and charcutiers producing mutton or lamb bacon and pancetta. It also has a place in substituting regular bacon where religious beliefs do not permit the consumption of pork.

This recipe uses the breast cut of lamb, equivalent to the belly of a pig, with its thick marbling of fat. The cut is relatively inexpensive, usually cheaper than lamb leg and roughly comparable with pork belly. It is often readily available at the butcher.

Lamb is usually slaughtered at less than 1 year old. Hogget is a sheep which has been raised to 1–2 years old and will have more flavour than lamb. The strongest flavours will come from mutton which is often 2–3 years old. The strong flavour of mutton can put off some consumers. It is a delicious meat though, with considerable flavour and well worth seeking out when it is available. It is possible to experiment with stronger spice blends with the older meat. Sumac, lemon zest and dried thyme, oregano, rosemary or mint can all work well incorporated into the cure in varying proportions, as does the North African spice blend ras al hanout. Use approximately ¼–½ tsp of any of these, added to the basic recipe that follows.

Sheep can have high levels of certain branched-chain fatty acids, such as 4-Methyloctanoic acid and 4-Ethyloctanoic acid, which can give the meat a strong 'mutton' flavour that is distinctive from that of other species. Lamb meat contains significantly lower levels of these fatty acids than those of older animals, which sometimes leads to greater consumer acceptance.

Mutton is tougher than lamb, with a lower moisture content. A larger cut may be preferable, with a smaller surface area to volume ratio. For both mutton and lamb, allow a curing time of around 2–3 days per kilogram (just under 1–1½ days per pound).

To smoke the meat after curing, follow the instructions on page 225 for smoked bacon and ham. Smoking helps to remove moisture from the meat which, along with the salt and sugar cure, helps to preserve it for longer as well as providing extra flavour.

INGREDIENTS

**Lamb breast, weighing
approximately 1.5kg/3lb 3oz**

200g/7oz pure dried vacuum (PDV) salt

20g/¾oz soft brown or golden sugar

2.5ml/½ tsp ground coriander

5ml/1 tsp crushed black pepper

Curing Salt #1, 2.5g/¹⁄₁₆oz per 1 kg/2.2lb of meat, optional (see the notes on pages 16–19 and always follow the manufacturer's instructions)

1 First, rinse the lamb (or mutton) and pat it dry with a kitchen towel. Run a flexible knife between the meat and the rib to debone it, and trim any loose scraps of fat or lean meat to give a good, even shape.

2 Weigh out and mix the PDV salt, sugar, coriander and black pepper together well. If using the curing salt, mix it in very thoroughly, always following the supplier's instructions regarding quantity as it can be harmful if used in excess.

3 Place the lamb into a strong plastic zip-lock bag or vacuum pouch. Pour in the cure mixture, ensuring that the meat is covered evenly on all sides. Clip or tie the top of the bag as the cure will draw water out from the meat to create a small quantity of brine.

4 Keep the curing meat in the refrigerator at a temperature of 3–5°C/37–41°F. It should remain there for up to 5 days and the bag should be shaken or stirred up each day to redistribute and rub in the cure evenly across the sides of the meat. It is important that the meat stays under temperature control until it takes up sufficient salt.

5 After 5 days, remove the meat from the bag and rinse off the cure with clean water. The meat can look a little darker after curing and may feel firmer due to the moisture lost into the cure mixture. Leave the meat to soak in fresh water for 30 minutes then drain it and pat it dry with a paper towel.

6 The meat should be hung on a bacon comb to dry slightly. Keep it in a cool, dark place for a minimum of 24 hours. It can be hung for longer periods of time and will continue to lose moisture though unlike cured pork products, the flavour of cold lamb fat is not always pleasant.

TO SERVE When you are ready to serve it, slice the lamb bacon into rashers using a sharp knife or a meat slicer. For best results, only slice as much as you need each time, as the bacon will keep best this way. Grill, broil or fry the bacon and serve warm.

SEASONAL LAMB

While, in the Northern hemisphere, lamb is often associated with Easter, the best time to enjoy it is actually several months later, at Christmas. The year's new lambs will have had time to grow by then.

DRY-CURED RACK OF LAMB

This is cooked and cured, and so is closer in method to a bacon recipe. Roast lamb is delicious but dry-curing takes it to a whole new level, with the salt locking moisture into the meat as it cooks to create a beautifully tender supper.

This recipe is inspired by Norwegian Pinnekjøtt, which is a cured and dried rib of lamb or mutton, often eaten at Christmas. The festive period is the best season for lamb in Northern Europe. By then the spring lambs have just reached a suitable age for slaughter. The Norwegian recipe involves curing the lamb rack in salt and sugar before hanging it to dry. The dried meat can then be soaked in water for a couple of days to remove some of the salt. Rather than roasting, it is sometimes steamed for up to 2 hours on a bed of stripped birch twigs. The twigs support the meat, keeping it out of the boiling water in the pan below.

Brining or dry-salting meat allows the salt to penetrate to the centre where it will trap moisture and prevent it from evaporating during cooking. This is particularly useful where a cut or type of meat is prone to drying, such as turkey, which can be made incredibly succulent by brining ahead of roasting. Lamb ribs have a good deal of fat which can protect them from drying but here enhances the flavour of the meat.

This dish also works well with North African and Middle Eastern spices such as sumac and ras al hanout, as well as traditional European accompaniments of rosemary, thyme, garlic and mint.

To experiment with these flavours, add half a teaspoon of the herbs or spices to the cure mixture before it is rubbed onto the lamb. The stronger flavours of the additional spices work well with the meat from older sheep, like hogget or mutton, which have a much more intense taste.

You can save yourself some time in preparing the lamb by asking your butcher to 'French trim' the rack. The tough membrane which covers the ribs is scored down the length of the bone and the fat and connective tissue is peeled off slowly to reveal the ends of the rib. There are usually a few scraps of tissue left on the bone and this is scraped off to neaten up the rack. Even if your butcher is trimming your rack, check over the ends of the bone and remove any loose scraps of meat or fat as they can become tough and very dark after the meat has been cured and cooked.

INGREDIENTS

Rack of lamb, weighing
approximately 700g/1lb 9oz

100g/3½oz pure dried vacuum (PDV) salt

7g/¼oz soft brown sugar

1.5ml/¼ tsp ground black pepper

Curing Salt #1, 2.5g/¹⁄₁₆oz per 1 kg/2.2lb of meat,
optional (see the notes on pages 16–19 and always
follow the manufacturer's instructions)

1 Rinse the rack of lamb and pat it dry with a kitchen towel. You can ask your butcher to French-trim the rack or do it yourself, scoring along each rib and removing the tough membrane. If it has not been removed, peel it back from the ribs and trim it to reveal up to 5cm/2in of exposed bone. Scrape the bones with a sharp knife to clean them and remove any traces of the meat, fat or membrane.

2 Weigh out the PDV salt, sugar and pepper as well as the curing salt, if using. Curing Salt #1 is used for meat that will be cooked rather than air-dried. The quantity of all the cure ingredients should be adjusted according to the quantity of meat used. Always measure the quantity of curing salt accurately and make sure it is well mixed into the other cure ingredients. See the notes on pages 16–19 for advice on the safe use of curing salt.

3 Place the rack of lamb into a plastic zip-lock bag or vacuum pouch. Pour in the cure, ensuring that the rack is covered evenly on all sides. Seal, clip or tie the top of the bag as the cure will draw water out from the meat, and place it immediately in the refrigerator. The lamb should be kept in the refrigerator at a temperature of 3–5°C/37–41°F as it cures. It should remain in the cure for 2 days. It may be left for a little longer, but it will continue to become saltier with time. Rub the cure over the meat each day to ensure even uptake of the salt.

4 Once the lamb has cured for 2 days, remove it from the bag or tub and wash off any excess cure. It should look darker at this point and will feel much firmer as moisture has been drawn out. Leave it to soak in a bowl of clean water for 15 minutes then drain it and pat the lamb dry with some paper kitchen towel.

5 The lamb can be hung at a temperature of 5–10°C/41–50°F for a few days until needed. It will become drier the longer it is kept, but if it is dried for a long period, then it may need to be soaked before cooking.

6 When ready to cook, preheat the oven to 200°C/392°F/Gas mark 6. Place the lamb rack, fat side up, on a roasting tray and place it in the oven for 15–20 minutes, turning the heat down to 180°C/356°F/Gas mark 4 after the first 5 minutes have elapsed. The lamb should be nicely browned but still pink in the middle. The cooking time can be extended for another 10 minutes if you would like it more well done. Remove the lamb from the oven and allow it to rest on a board or plate, covered with foil, for 10 minutes.

TO SERVE carve off each cutlet with a sharp knife and serve, perhaps with mashed potato or boiled and buttered new potatoes. A light red wine with berry fruit and a little acidity, like Pinot Noir, works very well with this lamb dish.

5

CURED FISH & SMOKED FOODS

While not part of the typical charcuterie offering, these simple cured fish dishes use many of the techniques described elsewhere in the book. Rollmops and gravadlax are easy to prepare without special equipment, while smoked salmon presents a new challenge for the enthusiast willing to invest in a home smoker. Continuing this theme, the techniques for smoking meats such as bacon and ham are also covered here, along with recipes for some simple snacks: beef jerky, which was traditionally dried over a smoky fire, and a recipe for the not-dissimilar biltong, a very chewy dried meat originating from South Africa.

ROLLMOPS

These delicious cured herrings marry the sweetness of the fresh fish with crisp acidity and subtle saltiness, and take only a short time to prepare.

Like gravadlax, rollmops are sometimes associated with Scandinavia, however there is a strong tradition of serving cured herrings across many Northern and Eastern European countries. The type of cure used may vary from country to country, but the herring is considered with something verging on national pride in a number of nations. Brined herrings, or maatjes, can be found in the Netherlands. The rollmop, preserved in vinegar, is believed to have originated in Germany.

Perhaps the popularity of the herring owes something to the ubiquitous distribution of the fish. Herrings may be found in the North Atlantic and Pacific Oceans, as well as the North Sea and Baltic. Salted and pickled herrings are found wherever the fish have a history of being landed, their preservation being a necessity of their perishable nature.

The names pilchard, sardine and herring all refer to members of the Clupeidae family of oily fish, comprising hundreds of species, including the Atlantic herring (*Clupea harengus*) and the pilchard or sardine (*Sardina pilchardus*), a pilchard being the name often used for a mature sardine over 15cm/6in long. In Cornwall, England, the pilchard has undergone something of a revival following its rebranding as a 'Cornish sardine', and it was awarded a Protected Geographical Indication (PGI) status in European law.

Herring stocks in Europe had gone into decline forty years ago, but careful management to prevent over-fishing has seen some success. The Atlantic herring lives to around 12 years old but is mature by 4 years. At maturity they measure around 25 cm or nearly 10 inches, though Baltic herring can be smaller, less than 18 cm or up to 7 inches.

While it may appear perverse to recommend buying very fresh fish and then freezing it, it should be remembered that fish are particularly susceptible to parasitic worms. To avoid the risks posed by them, read the notes on pages 34–35 and freeze the fish at -20°C/-4°C for 24 hours before curing.

INGREDIENTS

3 very fresh sardines or herrings, frozen for at least 24 hours

1 onion

Carrot, cucumber and fresh dill, optional

27g/1oz salt

295ml/10fl oz white wine vinegar

1 tsp/5ml sugar, optional

1 The herrings should be frozen before curing them. Thaw them in the refrigerator then scrape the sides of the herring gently with the back of a knife to remove any scales.

2 Slit open the belly and, using your finger, pull out the intestines. Cut out the dorsal fin on the back by slicing around it with a filleting knife. Wash the fish in clean water, removing any traces of the guts from the cavity.

3 To 'butterfly' the herring, use a flexible filleting knife to cut around the head. The cut should be made just behind the gills and the pectoral (side) but do not cut through the spine. Lay the herring on its back and pull the head upwards, gently separating the fillet from the head, spine and ribs. Rinse the fillet again in clean water. Check the fillet for bones and remove any that are found.

4 Peel and slice the onion into thin strips. With the skin side down, roll a handful of onion into the centre of the herring fillet. Other ingredients, such as matchstick-thin slices of carrot or cucumber, or some finely chopped dill, could also be added.

5 Roll the herring fillet up to enclose the filling and secure it with a cocktail stick or toothpick. Repeat with the other herring fillets.

6 Next make a brine by dissolving the salt in the wine vinegar. A sprinkling of sugar can also be added, according to taste.

7 Place the rollmops into a non-reactive bowl and pour the vinegar-brine over them, ensuring that they are completely submerged. Cover the bowl and keep it in the fridge for 1–2 days before serving. Rollmops can be refrigerated for a couple of weeks.

TO SERVE Rollmops make a delicious snack or light lunch and are very good served on open sandwiches with dill, mustard or mayonnaise.

FRESH FISH

It is possible to make these rollmops with either herring or sardines but, regardless of the species, make sure the fish is very fresh, carrying only the clean aroma of the sea, for it will be only lightly cured. If the herrings begin to spoil before being filleted and cured, the texture will be lost and the taste impaired.

GRAVADLAX

Salmon cured in dill, salt and sugar is as delicious as it is simple to prepare, and makes a great starter or canapé. Also referred to as gravlax or gravlaks, gravadlax was probably the first introduction I had to curing and has remained a firm favourite ever since. I often start preparing some gravadlax a few days before Christmas.

Gravadlax has a beautiful, distinctive appearance: the salt and sugar in the cure removes water from the fillets of salmon, leaving jewel-like almost translucent flesh, contrasting beautifully with the deep green of the dill. The recipe can trace its origins to the Vikings, who would have cured fish in salt to preserve it for the long Scandinavian winter or to provide sustenance as they sailed out to raid or to trade across the seas.

Gravadlax is best served with the honey and mustard dressing. It can become a simple summer lunch by serving it with some slices of dark rye bread or crispbreads for a lighter alternative. Add pickled gherkins, finely sliced onion and tomato, crisp lettuce and cream cheese to assemble various types of smørrebrød – a kind of open sandwich. If you are not serving the gravadlax with sparkling wine, a crisp lager-style beer makes a good alternative or a glass of akvavit – a clear caraway-flavoured schnapps – which should be served very cold, straight from the freezer.

The sugar plays a more significant role in the cure in this recipe than in many of the meat dishes prepared in this book, and the flavour is noticeably sweeter. To get the balance right on the cure I have used roughly equal quantities of sugar and salt, but am ever-so-slightly more generous with the sugar. You may wish to play around with the ratio of salt to sugar according to personal preference, but I would keep the total weight the same and advise not changing either quantity by more than 1/10th of the quantity stated in the recipe.

Substituting unrefined granulated sugar in place of the refined white variety adds the pleasing hint of molasses to the finished dish. It is not possible to use artificial sweeteners in place of the sugar and only coarse salt should be used here, as fine pure dried vacuum salt will make the fish tough and unpleasantly salty.

For those of you used to buying dill in small 27g/1oz packets in the supermarket, you will need at least four or five packs. It is the quantity of dill, and the freshness of the fish, which really makes this dish and you should not scrimp on either.

INGREDIENTS

A side of salmon, weighing 1kg/2lb 2oz – very fresh, skin on

A large bunch of fresh dill (reserving a quarter for the sauce and garnish)

55g/1¾oz coarse sea salt or fleur de sel

60g/2oz granulated sugar

Freshly ground black pepper

FOR THE HONEY AND MUSTARD SAUCE

30ml/2 tbsp honey
30ml/2 tbsp Dijon mustard
15ml/1 tbsp soft brown sugar
15–30ml/1–2 tbsp sunflower oil
15–30ml/1–2 tbsp cider vinegar
Dill (reserved from earlier)

1 If preparing a whole fish, scrape the sides of the fish with a knife to remove the scales. Slice each side of the head just below the gills and then chop through the spine. Working from the head end, run the blade of a filleting knife down the spine, running it around the dorsal fin on the back. Once the knife reaches the spine, run it across the rib bones to free the fillet. Repeat with the second fillet.

2 Freeze the side fillets of salmon for at least 24 hours at -20°C/-4°F and thaw in the refrigerator before commencing the cure. (See the section on food saftey on pages 34–35 for more details.) You can keep one half of the salmon in the freezer for a later date while curing the other half. Dry the salmon by patting it with a paper towel. Trim the fish into two equal-sized rectangles.

3 Run your hand gently along the surface of each fillet; if there are any pin bones, remove them by hand, gripping them between your fingers or between a finger and a table knife. If it is not possible to grip them, try using a very clean pair of tweezers.

4 Reserve approximately quarter of the dill for the sauce and to use as a garnish; keep it in a sealed container in the refrigerator until it is needed. It is possible to make the sauce in advance but the garnish should be chopped immediately before use.

5 To make the cure, chop the dill finely using a chef's knife in a steady rocking action, working back and forth until it is very fine and evenly sized. Mix the chopped dill with the salt, sugar and freshly ground black pepper.

6 Scatter a handful of the dill and cure mixture onto the centre of a sheet of clingfilm or food wrap, roughly four times the size of the salmon fillets. Place one of the fillets skin-side down onto the cure. Reserving another handful of the dill and cure mixture, scatter the rest on the top of the fillet.

7 Sandwich the second fillet on top of it, this time skin-side up. Scatter the final handful of the dill and cure mixture on top of the salmon.

8 Gather the edges of the clingfilm and fold them over to make a small parcel. Place the salmon parcel into a dish and put a small weight, such as a plate, on top to gently press it. The gravadlax should be kept in the fridge while it is curing. Turn the parcel over twice each day, at roughly 12-hour intervals. It should be cured for approximately 36 hours; 24 hours at the very least and no more than 48 hours as the fish will become tough and usually very salty. A small quantity of liquid brine will collect around the fish. This is normal and should not be removed as it is essential to get the cure into the salmon.

9 When the gravadlax has cured for the required time, unwrap the parcel and brush off the excess cure. It is alright to leave some traces of the dill on the surface of the fish but the flavour will be better if fresh dill is chopped as a garnish.

10 To make the sauce, put the honey, mustard and sugar into a small jar or dish. Thin the mixture with the oil and vinegar and stir it well. Just before you are ready to serve, finely chop and add the reserved dill. Cover the sauce and keep refrigerated until needed.

TO SERVE Only slice the gravadlax once you are ready to serve it. Use a very sharp knife and cut it in fine slices at 90 degrees to the length of the fillet. If not using immediately, wrap in clingfilm and keep covered in the refrigerator for up to 3 days.

HOT-SMOKED & COLD-SMOKED SALMON

Smoked salmon is typically prepared one of two ways: hot-smoked and flaky; or cold-smoked with a clean flavour and firm flesh. Both techniques are delicious and reasonably easy to prepare at home. Regardless of the method employed to smoke the fish, the preparation of the salmon and the curing of the fillet is the same.

Cold-smoked salmon is not cooked during its preparation, as the temperature does not exceed 30°C/86°F during smoking. This can be achieved in one of two ways – either by using a 'cold smoke generator' such as those fired by wood dust and powered by a small candle, or alternatively by having a long pipe between the smoking chamber and the point at which the smoke is generated. This allows the smoke to cool to the required temperature.

Fill a cold-smoke generator such as the ProQ Cold Smoke Generator with oak wood dust. Alternatively, a Bradley cold-smoke generator can be used, along with their proprietary oak briquettes. The cold-smoke generator should be placed in, or connected to, a large cardboard box, big enough to hold the salmon at least 20cm/8in above the source of the smoke.

Cold-smoking must be carried out on a cool day and the humidity should be neither very low nor excessively high. It is undoubtedly a riskier operation as the temperatures used allow the growth of harmful bacteria in the fish. For this reason salmon is typically cured using salt and sugar before cold-smoking it, if it to be eaten without cooking. Some cold-smoked fish is intended to be cooked before eating; including some types of smoked haddock for one example.

For hot-smoking, the temperature of the smoke is higher, exceeding 70°C/158°F. This both flavours and cooks the fish, so the fillet will flake just as though it was grilled. Hot-smoked salmon can be served warm, straight from the smoker, or chilled and served cold.

Hot-smoked salmon can be prepared quite easily using a lidded barbecue. No charcoal is needed, as the wood chips provide both the heat and the smoke. (See pages 32–33 for additional information about the smokers.)

There are several different types of wood available for smoking, but alder or oak are perhaps most commonly associated with smoked salmon. Cherry and apple are also suitable, having mild flavours, but longer smoking times may be required as a result, to impart the necessary smokiness. Coniferous woods such as fir, pine and spruce, which contain a lot of resin, are not suitable for smoking foods. They will spit when heated and the turpenes they contain can taint the meat. Neither are any woods which have been treated with preservative chemicals. Use wood chips that are sold as being suitable for smoking foods or barbecuing. If gathering your own, use wood from a known source, free from chemical contaminants, and where the wood type has been reliably identified.

TO CURE THE SALMON

**A side of salmon, weighing 1kg/2lb 2oz –
very fresh, skin on**

100g/3½oz fleur de sel (sea salt)

85g/3oz golden caster sugar

1.5ml/¼ tsp ground black pepper

1 To prepare the side of salmon from a whole fish, first scrape the sides of the fish with a knife to remove all the scales. Rinse the fish in cold water and rinse the chopping board. Slice each side of the head just below the gills and chop through the spine. Run a flexible filleting knife down the spine, from the head to the tail, with a gentle cutting action. The knife should make contact with the spine as it goes in near the head, and it is simply a matter of following down to the tail, removing the rib bones from the fillet as you go. Cut around the dorsal fin on the back once the knife reaches it. Turn the fish over and repeat on the other side.

2 If cold-smoking the fish, freeze the side fillets of salmon first, for at least 24 hours at -20°C/-4°F to kill off any parasites that it may be carrying, then thaw it in the refrigerator before curing. Dry the salmon by patting it with a paper towel. The side fillet can be used whole or chopped in half to give two roughly equal-sized portions.

3 Run your hand gently along the surface of each fillet. Remove any pin bones where you find them, using your thumb against the blunt edge of the knife

to tweezer them out. With the skin side down, remove the skin using the filleting knife. Work along the length of the fish with a firm but gentle slicing action. The fillet should easily be freed from the skin.

4 Prepare the cure by mixing together the salt, sugar and ground black pepper. Coat the side of salmon evenly with the cure mixture, loosely roll it and place it in a plastic food bag or tub in the fridge. A squeeze of lemon juice, or small amount of grated lemon zest, can be added if you like to give the fish a hint of citrus flavour but avoid adding lemon juice directly to the flesh of the fish as the acidity can cause the raw salmon to take on a 'cooked' appearance.

5 Place the salmon in the refrigerator for 24 hours. It is normal for a small amount of brine to form around the fish. Turn the salmon over once or twice during curing to ensure that the salt is taken up evenly.

6 Remove the salmon from the bag and rinse the excess cure off by dipping briefly it in cold water. The fish should be left at room temperature for 4–6 hours for the surface to dry. Once this is done, the fish is ready to smoke, either by hot or cold smoking.

TO HOT-SMOKE SALMON

Place several handfuls of wood smoking chips and some sawdust into a small, lidded barbecue, scattering it around evenly. No charcoal should be used as the fish will be cooked by the smoke.

The grill should be at least 10cm/4in above the wood chips, but further away if possible. Use a kitchen blowtorch to light the sawdust in several places, and replace the lid on the barbecue to allow the smoke to fill. Once the air temperature reaches 50°C/122°F, the fish can be placed in the barbecue.

Place the salmon on the grill rack and put this in the makeshift smoker, replacing the lid to allow the smoke to collect. Check the air temperature inside the smoker periodically using a digital thermometer. The internal temperature of the fish must reach at least 71°C/160°F for a continuous period of at least half an hour. This temperature should ideally be towards the end of smoking. The temperature should not exceed 80°C/176°F, however, as this can dry the fish out too much. If it is too hot, lift the lid of the barbecue slightly to allow it to cool or, if possible, increase the height between the fish and the wood chips. The fire can also be damped down by splashing a little cold water on it.

As they are burnt down, the smoking chips should be topped up whenever necessary. Aim to hot-smoke the fish for between 4 and 6 hours in total, turning it two or three times during smoking.

The longer the time that it is smoked for, the more intense the smoky flavour of the fish will be. To prolong the smoking time, however, you should extend the period at cooler temperatures at the start of smoking, rather than by extending the time at higher temperatures. A suggested smoking cycle is outlined below:

1 Try to maintain the temperature at 55–60°C/130–158°F for 2–4 hours initially, or longer but up to a maximum of 6 hours, for a smokier flavour.

2 Next bring the temperature up to 70–75°C/158–167°F during 1–1½ hours. Ensure that the internal temperature of the fish reaches a minimum of 71°C/160°F when checked with a probe thermometer for at least 30 minutes.

3 Remove the fish from the smoker and, unless eating it immediately, cool it quickly to below 6°C/43°F. The hot-smoked salmon will have taken on a golden-brown colour and will be cooked through. It can be eaten straight away or refrigerated and used up within 5 days. It can be eaten whole or flaked as an ingredient in salads and soups.

Where an actual smoker is available, the smoking cycle is the same, but the temperatures should be easier to maintain accurately.

TO COLD-SMOKE SALMON

Prepare your cold-smoke generator, light the smoker and place it in the box. The smoke temperature should be around 11–20°C/52–68°F.

Place the cured salmon on a grill rack above the smoker, or hang it using some butcher's hooks from a pole pushed through the walls of the box, replacing the lid to allow the smoke to collect. Check the air temperature inside the smoker periodically using a digital thermometer. It should not exceed 30°C/86°F.

Smoke the fish for 8–12 hours, checking the smoker periodically during this time and topping up the wood if necessary. The longer the time the fish is smoked, the stronger the flavour.

One the fish has been smoked, cool it quickly then carve into thin slices and serve immediately. Keep any unused cold-smoked salmon covered in the refrigerator for up to 5 days.

JERKY

These tender strips of dried tender beef topside, marinated in salt, sugar and soy sauce, make the perfect bar snack or a useful and versatile ingredient for the campfire kitchen.

Originating in the Americas, the word jerky is believed to be derived from the Quechuan word *ch'arki*, meaning 'salted dried meat'. The Quechua people were the indigenous inhabitants of the Peruvian Andes in South America and the direct descendants of the Inca. It would have been an ideal way to preserve meat for journeys and times when fresh food was scarce.

Native North American Indians are also known to have made a type of jerky from the meat of the bison, or buffalo. Every part of the carcass of a slaughtered animal was used and the scraps of meat were preserved by salting and drying, sometimes over an open fire so that the smoke infused into the jerky, flavouring it and helping to dry it. Excess fat would be trimmed off prior to preparing it, to prevent it from spoiling by becoming rancid.

These cured meat products have a long tradition of being associated with pioneering adventurers, throwing themselves into the unknown in hope of a better future. At the time of the gold rush, as the descendants of American settlers migrated across the country, it is believed that they are likely to have encountered the jerky through their trades with the native tribes. The dried meat made the perfect food ration for their journey west, being durable, nutritious and easy to stow in their saddlebags.

This jerky recipe is easy to follow at home without the need for special equipment such as a meat dehydrator or biltong box, instead using a standard oven. The door of the oven is propped open and a low heat setting is used to ensure that the meat dries rather than bakes.

The smoke has been omitted here in favour of the salty and savoury flavours of dark soy sauce. Additional piquancy is provided care of a little white pepper and an optional dash of Worcestershire sauce, a thin, dark sauce made from fermented anchovies. Alternatively, a little Pontack sauce can be used instead. This is a traditional but rarely encountered sauce, often used to accompany game, such as venison. Hard, if not impossible, to find, it can easily be made at home from ripe elderberries if those grow locally, and lasts almost indefinitely, getting a little better in flavour every year – you'll find the method on page 219. Once tasted, it is likely to become a firm favourite of the kitchen cupboard.

The recipe should yield a jerky which is chewy but with a slight tenderness, compared to the dryness of the mouthfeel of the biltong recipe. It should keep for up to about one month, or longer if the meat remains in the oven for longer to dry. I find it a useful thing to take camping or hiking as it can withstand storage out of the refrigerator and can be chopped and added to simple egg and pasta dishes as they are prepared on a camping stove. As a ready-to-eat food, it is also suitable to keep close to hand as a snack to restore flagging energy levels.

INGREDIENTS

**Beef topside, weighing
approximately 500g/1lb 1oz**

7g/¼oz pure dried vacuum (PDV) salt

1.5ml/¼ tsp golden sugar

5ml/1 tsp ground white pepper

15ml/1 tbsp olive oil

15ml/1 tbsp soy sauce

**5ml/1 tsp Worcestershire sauce or
Pontack sauce, optional**

1 Find the direction of the muscle fibres in the beef and cut it into 1cm/⅓in thick strips at 90 degrees across the grain. Trim off any fat and place the meat into a plastic food bag.

2 Weigh out the salt, adjusting the quantity as necessary for the weight of the meat. Add the salt, sugar and pepper to the meat.

3 Measure out the oil, soy sauce and Worcestershire or Pontack sauce (if using) and add them to the meat. Massage the meat with the marinade for a minute before placing the bag into the refrigerator to allow the flavours to infuse. It should be left for 12 hours. Massage the marinade into the meat once or twice during this time.

4 Remove the bag from the refrigerator and leave the meat at room temperature for an hour until it loses its chill. Preheat the oven to 80°C/177°F.

5 Place the meat onto a rack on a roasting tray, leaving plenty of space between the strips to allow them to dry. Place the tray into the oven and leave the door ajar to allow the hot air to escape. Dry the jerky in the oven for up to 4 hours. It will feel noticeably firmer once it is dry.

6 Once it is ready, remove the jerky from the oven. Leave it to cool in a dry place.

TO SERVE When ready to serve, use a very sharp knife to slice the strips thinly along the grain of the meat. Chop the jerky into small pieces. It will last around a month if stored in a cool, dry place.

PONTACK SAUCE

Take 500g/1lb 1oz of fresh elderberries stripped from their stalks, which must be removed. Wash the berries and place them into an ovenproof dish. They should be baked for around 3 hours at 140°C/284°F/ Gas mark 1 until they begin to release their juice. Squeeze out as much juice as possible, into a pan, through a fine sieve or a square of muslin.

Add 200ml/7fl oz of cider vinegar to the strained juice, along with one finely sliced onion, a pinch of mace or nutmeg, and a couple of cloves and allspice berries, and bring to the boil. Turn down the heat slightly and continue to simmer for 10 minutes.

Remove the pan from the heat and strain off the liquid into a sterilised jar. Seal the lid on the jar while it is still warm.

Label it, and keep in a dark cupboard for at least 4 months before opening. The flavour will continue to improve with age.

BILTONG

Drier and often more chewy than beef jerky, biltong makes an excellent snack meat, and is easily prepared by marinating and drying beef, infused with the aromatic citrus aromas of ground coriander seed.

Biltong originates in southern Africa, where the warm summer conditions traditionally required the meat to be salted and dried to prevent it from spoiling. The meat is also marinated in vinegar which helps to acidify it, preventing the growth of harmful bacteria. It is believed that meat was preserved in a similar way by the indigenous people of modern-day South Africa before Dutch-speaking settlers adopted the technique.

Biltong gets much of its flavour from the coriander seed which is used to flavour the marinade. In addition to the lemony fragrance it imparts to the meat, the seeds are packed with essential oil containing a range of organic compounds, notably linalool, which is known to have powerful anti-microbial properties.

One of the key textural attributes of the biltong, its famed chewiness, depends on the way that the meat is cut. The strips of beef are sliced along the grain of the muscle fibres, before they are dried. Afterwards, when the biltong is cut before serving, it can be sliced against the grain, at 90 degrees to the first cut, which makes it easier to chew. Alternatively, it can be sliced along the grain again which exposes lengths of connective tissue and makes it chewier.

As it is dry, biltong doesn't usually lend itself well to cooking in the way that hams and salamis do. It can, however, be grated finely to make a delicious and versatile seasoning ingredient, adding savoury umami flavours to a wide variety of dishes. The grated biltong should be sieved before use in this way, to remove the sinewy connective tissue. It can liven up macaroni cheese, either added to the sauce or sprinkled on the top at the end of cooking, as well as making a great garnish for potato salad or a topping for small canapes such as crostini.

Biltong can be made in a 'biltong box', which is a kind of dryer, or desiccator, used to remove moisture from the meat. Often the box will have a small light bulb to provide a heat source and a fan to circulate air. It is possible to make delicious biltong without any special equipment though, and this recipe makes use of a fan oven to provide both heat and air movement. The temperature of the oven is set quite low and the door left slightly ajar to avoid cooking the meat rather than drying it.

When storing the biltong after it is made, make sure that it is not left in a damp place as this will encourage the growth of surface moulds and will cause the meat to spoil. The recipe does not make use of the curing salts featured in some of the other recipes, and adequate salting and refrigeration of the meat while it is marinating are therefore important to ensure quality and safety.

It may be possible to reduce the salt level a little, according to taste. This can easily be achieved by reducing the time that the beef spends in the marinade from 4 hours down to 2.

INGREDIENTS

Beef topside or silverside, weighing approximately 500g/1lb 1oz

15g/½oz pure dried vacuum (PDV) salt

5ml/1 tsp coriander seeds

5ml/1 tsp crushed black pepper

5ml/1 tsp dried chilli flakes, optional

2.5ml/½ tsp golden sugar

15ml/1 tbsp red wine vinegar

1 Weigh out the salt, adjusting the quantity as necessary for the exact weight of the meat. Lightly crush the coriander seeds using a pestle and mortar. Add to the salt along with the black pepper, chilli flakes and sugar. Mix together well.

2 Cut the beef into strips running along the grain of the meat. This can be recognised by looking at the direction that the muscle fibres and connective tissue are aligned. The strips should be approximately 1cm/⅓in thick.

3 Place the sliced beef into a plastic food bag and pour in the spice mixture. Gently massage it onto the meat, ensuring that all the sides are evenly coated.

4 Pour in the wine vinegar and massage it for a minute before placing the bag into the refrigerator for 2–4 hours, to allow the meat to take up the flavours of the marinade. Mix up the contents of the bag once or twice during this time.

5 Remove the bag from the refrigerator. Take out the meat and brush off most of the excess marinade. The odd bit of coriander or chilli left on the outside of the meat will not hurt though, and makes the biltong look pleasingly rustic.

6 Preheat the oven to a low temperature, about 80°C/177°F/Gas mark ½. Place the meat onto a rack on a roasting tray, leaving plenty of space between the strips to allow them to dry properly. Place the tray into the oven and leave the door ajar to allow the hot air to escape. The drying biltong should be checked periodically until completely dry. This may take up to 4 hours, though thinly sliced strips of meat will dry more quickly than larger pieces.

7 Remove the biltong from the oven and leave it to cool for several hours, either on a metal rack or by hanging it. It should not be refrigerated nor covered.

TO SERVE When ready to serve, use a very sharp knife to slice the strips thinly either across their width or along their length to give a chewier texture. The biltong should be dry all the way to the centre. Reject any strips which have not dried properly at the core or which appear to be discoloured.

Slice as much biltong as you need and store any unused strips in a cool, dry place, away from insects and other pests. If properly dried they will keep almost indefinitely but use the biltong within a few months for the best quality.

SMOKING CURED OR DRIED MEATS

Enhance the flavour of your home-cured bacon and ham with several hours of cold-smoking over oak wood chips. The cold-smoking will impart a delicious aroma of wood smoke to the surface of the meat. The smoke also has a mild preservative effect but this cannot be relied upon to make the meat safe unless it is carried out in conjunction with curing and afterwards partially drying the meat. For instructions on how to cure bacon, see the recipes on pages 168–179 as this will be the starting point for success with smoking.

It is easy to smoke bacon using a cold-smoke generator placed inside a cardboard box. The small 'maze' type smoke generators made by ProQ are a good and cost-effective way of launching into home smoking and the wood dust they use will burn for up to 10 hours. It is, however, also possible to use items more likely to be found around the home, such as a small lidded barbecue. The crucial thing in smoking meat is to ensure adequate temperature control. The temperature for cold-smoking should not exceed 30°C/86°F to avoid cooking the meat. This can be achieved by having sufficient height between the smoke generator and the meat or, if necessary, by damping down the wood chips by spraying a little water on them.

Different wood types will have different flavours. Wood from fruit trees such as cherry and apple, which works very well with pork, have sweet and mild flavours and may require longer smoking times. At the milder end of the scale, we also find beech,

silver birch and maple, which is sweet-flavoured. Oak has a medium to strong flavour and is frequently used for smoking meat. Hickory, which works very well with bacon, imparts a much stronger smoke flavour so the smoking time may be reduced slightly. The various wood types can be mixed to create a unique smoke blend, using a small amount of hickory tempered by milder tasting woods such as oak or apple. It is also possible to buy old whiskey barrels, made of wood, once they have reached the end of their working life, and chips or shavings from these will impart wonderful aromatic qualities to the meat.

Resinous woods such as pine are not suitable for smoking foods, and you must never use wood which has been treated with a preservative or paint. Old pallets and furniture are not suitable for smoking!

TO SMOKE BACON

1 The bacon can be dry-cured (see pages 268–171) or brined according to the recipe on pages 175–179 and then hung at 5–10°C/41–50°F for 1–2 days to allow the pellicle to form. This is the glossy coat that forms naturally on the surface of the bacon and it will allow a good amount of smoke flavour to settle on the surface of the meat.

2 Fill a cold-smoke generator with hickory or oak wood dust, chips or briquettes, according to the manufacturer's instructions. Alternatively, place some wood dust and chips in the base of a lidded barbecue.

3 If using a cold-smoke generator, it should be placed in a large cardboard box that is big enough to hang the bacon. Light the wood dust or chips in one or two places and close the lid. The smoke temperature should ideally be kept around 11–20°C/52–68°F. For best results, smoke the bacon on a cool, dry day.

4 Place the bacon on a grill rack above the smoker. If using a box, the bacon can instead be hung on a butcher's hook or bacon comb on a pole pushed through the walls of the box. Replace the lid and allow the smoke to collect around the bacon. Check the air temperature inside the smoker from time to time using a digital thermometer. It should not exceed a maximum of 30°C/86°F – the lid of the smoker can be opened slightly if it begins to heat up too much.

5 Smoke the bacon for at least 6 hours in total, though it may need longer for a smokier flavour. Rather than overdoing the smoke, if it needs more it is best to cool the bacon in the refrigerator overnight and smoke it again the next day for another 6 hours. The wood should be topped up as necessary.

6 Once the bacon has been smoked, to a satisfactory degree according to personal preference, it may appear to be a golden-brown colour on the rind, though this colour will become progressively darker the longer the meat is smoked for.

7 The bacon can be sliced and fried immediately after smoking, or kept in the fridger for up to 2 weeks.

TO SMOKE HAM

1 To prepare a ham for smoking, it should be cured in the refrigerator, packed in salt, for 2–3 days per kilogram or 2 pounds of meat, as described in the air-dried ham recipe on pages 38–43.

2 After curing, wash off the excess salt and smoke following the method described for bacon.

3 Smoke the ham twice, for up to 6 hours each time, after which it is wrapped in muslin and hung at 12–18°C/53–64°F. As described in the air-dried recipe, it should be hung until it loses at least one third of its initial weight, but can be sliced and eaten without cooking after this time.

4 For larger smoked air-dried hams in the style of prosciutto affumicato or speck from the Tyrol region, the cut is bigger with a longer curing time, and so the ham may require a several successive periods of smoking to take up a good amount of flavour and develop a rich golden sheen on the surface.

TO SMOKE KIELBASA

1 To hot-smoke kielbasa the smoke should reach a temperature of 71–75°C/160–167°F, and the sausages should remain in the hot smoke until their internal temperature reaches 71°C/160°F when probed with a digital thermometer.

2 To cold-smoke kielbasa use a temperature of 11–18°C/52–64°F for 4–6 hours. They must be hung to complete the curing process after smoking.

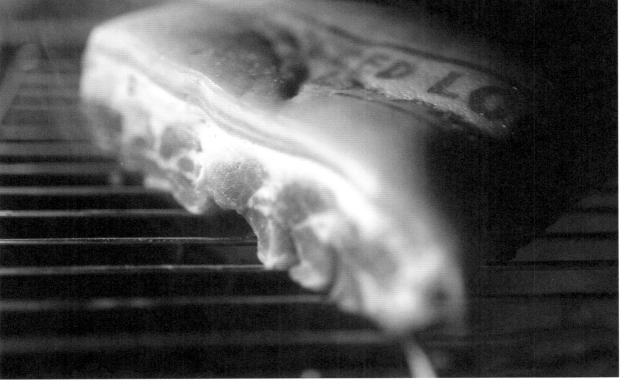

GLOSSARY

Bioprotective cultures Microbes which are used as starter cultures and which have the ability to outgrow or inhibit the growth of harmful microorganisms. Some are chosen as starter cultures due to their known ability to inhibit certain harmful bacteria by producing inhibitory substances, called bacteriocins.

Brining The curing of meat, or fish, by placing it in a tank containing a salt solution of a specified concentration. Salt will diffuse into the flesh from the brine. Industrial brining may also make use of a brine pump to inject the salt water into the product more quickly. 'Live cures' such as the Wiltshire cure also contain salt-tolerant cultures which help to fix the pink colour in meat and can have a protective effect by providing microbial competition to inhibit the growth of harmful bacteria.

Butcher's knot A knot used to secure a rolled joint of meat. For step-by-step instructions on how to tie this knot, see page 188.

Case hardening Excessive drying of the exterior of a cured product such as salami, often due to inadequate humidity control during drying. The dry case prevents the further loss of moisture from the core, resulting in high moisture which causes the product to spoil rapidly or allow the growth or survival of harmful microbes. It can be prevented by ensuring adequate relative humidity during drying to ensure slow and steady moisture loss from the product.

Casings Natural or synthetic materials designed to enclose sausages and salamis. Natural casings may be made of the intestines of cows, sheep or goats, while synthetic types may be manufactured from cellulose, collagen or plastic.

Cold-smoking The treatment of a cured meat or fish with smoke that has cooled by the time it reaches the smoking chamber. This will impart flavour and draw out moisture, but it does not cook the food being smoked. As a result cold-smoked meat and fish must either be cured before, or cooked after, smoking.

Cure This can either refer to a verb describing the process of preserving meat by salting and/or drying or a noun which describes the salt mixture used for this process.

Curing salts Sodium nitrate or nitrite added to a cure or brine to limit the growth of harmful bacteria and to promote the formation of red-pink pigments in cured meat.

Drying box A box usually made of wood for drying meat such as air-dried hams or biltong. This has holes to allow air to flow through the box and dry the meat, and may be protected by a fine mesh to keep pests, such as flying insects, out. Specially made biltong boxes will sometimes have a small light bulb in the base to act as a heat source or a small electric fan, though the same effect can be achieved with a fan oven on a low heat setting.

Dry-salting The curing of meat or fish by applying dry salt to the outside of the product rather than using a brine tank (see brining).

OPPOSITE 1 Coppa **2** Pepperoni salami **3** Rolled pancetta

Fermentation chamber A box or other vessel which is used to maintain temperature and humidity around a salami as it ferments.

Freezing Commonly used to preserve foods, freezing can also inactivate parasitic organisms, especially in fish, prior to curing. The correct duration at specified temperature is important.

Hot-smoking The treatment of a cured meat or fish with hot smoke to both impart flavour and cook the item being cured.

Hurdle technology Many traditional foods such as cheese and charcuterie products rely on 'hurdles' to prevent the growth of harmful bacteria in the food. Hurdles can include: pH or acidity, microbial competition by bioprotective cultures, salt, or temperature. It might be that individual hurdles taken in isolation would not be sufficient to inhibit the growth of harmful bacteria, but when used in combination they are more effective.

Microbial competition Competition occurs when a dominant population of one or more organisms, outgrow and/or inhibit a smaller number of harmful microorganisms. An example is the inhibition of harmful bacteria, such as *Listeria monocytogenes*, by dominant strains of starter bacteria added as a bioprotective culture. Microbial competition is one of the most significant contributors to food safety in many traditional foods which are based on hurdle technologies. Unlike acidity (pH), salt or water activity, it can be the hardest hurdle to quantify or predict as its effectiveness depends on many factors which are hard to measure during food manufacturing.

Parasites Organisms such as parasitic worms which are able to live on or within a host. The parasite uses them to provide shelter and food, often to the detriment of the host. Examples include Trichinella in pork or nematodes in fish. Parasites pose a hazard when making cured meat and fish dishes. They can be killed by freezing and maintaining the correct salt level and processing conditions.

Pathogens Harmful microorganisms which can cause human disease, including *Listeria monocytogenes* and *Clostridium botulinum*. Their presence in cured meats can be reduced or removed through observing good hygiene measures, following the correct process for each recipe, including specified temperatures and ingredients.

pH A measure of the acidity of a substance, reported on a scale from 1–14; pH7 is neutral and values less than this are acidic. pH may be monitored in salami production to ensure that the right acidity is achieved. The acidity has a protective effect on the cured meat, inhibiting the growth of pathogenic bacteria. pH also acts as an indicator of the growth of the cultures, which provide microbial competition.

Sear and shave A technique to kill harmful *E. coli* strains which may be present on the exterior of a whole cut of meat before mincing it. See page 67.

Starter cultures A mixture of bacteria which have protective effect during curing, providing microbial competition against less-desirable bacteria or influencing flavour and pigmentation of the meat.

Stuffer A device, motorised or hand-cranked, which is used to fill the casings in sausages and salamis. Some meat mincers will also have a stuffing funnel.

OPPOSITE 1 Small snacking salami sticks **2** Various cured salamis, sliced on the round **3** Coppa, marbled with delicious fat

SUPPLIERS

For sausage-making and butchery supplies, the details of some suppliers are provided below. The inclusion of a business on this list does not indicate an endorsement and other suppliers are available.

UNITED KINGDOM

Butchers Sundries
TruNet Packaging Services Ltd T/A Butchers-Sundries
Unit D Norman Court, Ivanhoe Business Park,
Ashby-De-La-Zouch, Leicestershire LE65 2UZ
Phone: 01530 411275
Email: info@butchers-sundries.com
Website: www.butchers-sundries.com

Sausagemaking.org
Swan Centre, Higher Swan Lane, Bolton BL3 3AQ
Phone: 0845 643 6915
Email: sales@sausagemaking.org
Website: www.sausagemaking.org

Smurfy's Home Curing Supplies
Phone: 01903 250240 or 07860 157107
Website: www.homecuring.co.uk

Weschenfelder Direct Ltd
10 Copeland Court, Forest Grove Business Park,
Riverside , Middlesbrough TS2 1RN
Phone: 01642 241 395
Email: rob.wesch@weschenfelder.co.uk
Website: www.weschenfelder.co.uk

EUROPE

www.startercultures.eu
Tussendek 70, 1034 TT Amsterdam, Netherlands
Phone: +31 (0)6-81255054
Email: info@starterculturen.nl
Website: www.starterculturen.nl, www.startercultures/eu

CANADA

Stuffers Supply Company
22958 Fraser Highway, Langley, BC V2Z 2T9
Phone: 1-800-615-4474
Email: sales@stuffers.com
Website: www.stuffers.com

UNITED STATES

Dirt Cheap Casings
201-A East Fifth Street, Washington, MO 63090
Phone: 262-960-2143
E-mail: info@dirtcheapcasings.com
Website: dirtcheapcasings.com

OPPOSITE 1 White *Penicillium* moulds dominate the surface of these traditional salamis **2** Pancetta, a cured slab of pork belly **3** Traditional cooked meats such as stuffed rolled pork belly are making a comeback on the deli counter

Natural Casing Co.
410 E. Railroad, Street Peshtigo WI 54157
Phone: (715) 582-3736
Email: info@naturalcasingco.com
Website: naturalcasingco.com

The Sausage Maker, Inc.
1500 Clinton St, Bldg 123, Buffalo, NY 14206-3099
Phone: (716) 824-5814
Email: customerservice@sausagemaker.com
Website: www.sausagemaker.com

AUSTRALIA

Butcher at Home
Unit 3/5 Inglis Court, Bundaberg QLD 4670
Phone: 1800 657 166
Email: sales@butcherathome.com.au
Website: www.butcherathome.com.au

Sausages Made Simple
118 Ireland St, West Melbourne VIC 3003
Phone: + 61 3 9329 4422
Email: enquiries@sausagesmadesimple.com.au
Website: www.sausagesmadesimple.com.au

Smoked and Cured
3/55 Radford Rd, Reservoir, Victoria 3073

OPPOSITE 1 Salami Toscano; the larger chunks of fat dispersed through the lean meat give the salami its unique texture **2** The different sizes and shapes of salamis make for a deliciously inviting retail display

Phone: 03 8592 8307
Email: info@smokedandcured.com.au
Website: www.smokedandcured.com.au

NEW ZEALAND

Dunninghams
655 Great South Road, Penrose, Auckland,
PO Box 12 572, Penrose, Auckland 1642
Phone: 09 525 8188
Email: sales@dunninghams.co.nz
Website: www.dunninghams.co.nz

Lewis Gray Ltd.
40G William Pickering Drive, North Harbour,
Albany, Auckland 0751
Postal Address:P O Box 302060
Auckland 0751
New Zealand
Phone: +64 9 415 3348
Email: sales@sausageingredients.co.nz
Website: sausageingredients.co.nz

New Zealand Casing Company
Site 30, Johnston Way
Whakatu, 4172
Hawke's Bay
New Zealand
Phone: +64 6 650 4140
Email: admin@nzcasings.co.nz
Website: http://nzcasings.co.nz

Oskar Butcher
Phone: 03-3849139 or 0274381783
Website: https://oskarbutcher.co.nz

INDEX

ABOUT THE AUTHOR

Having graduated with a degree in Biochemistry in 1999, Paul Thomas worked in the cheese industry for over a decade before becoming a dairy technologist and food safety adviser to dairy businesses across the world. Paul has taught cheesemaking courses at the School of Artisan Food and River Cottage, among many other highly regarded training centres. His first book, Home-Made Cheese, was published by Lorenz Books in 2016. Paul was also on the writing team who prepared the European Guide to Good Hygiene Practices in the Production of Artisanal Cheese and Dairy Products, a guide endorsed by the European Commission and published within the official journal of the EU. He is a consultant for the Guild of Fine Foods, and writes their 'delihelp' column. His research into charcuterie began when he started to make his own cured meats while working as a cheesemaker on a farm in South of England.

IMPORTANT NOTES

While the author has made all reasonable efforts to ensure the information in this book is accurate and up to date at the time of publication, anyone reading this book should note the following important points:

• Medical and bacteriological knowledge is frequently updated and the author and the publisher cannot and do not guarantee the accuracy or appropriateness of the contents of this book.
• Many food-poisoning bacteria can cause severe complications, or death, with the elderly, young children, pregnant women and the immunocompromised considered to be at greatest risk.
• *Listeria monocytogenes* is able to grow under refrigerated conditions in some ready to eat foods including pate and cured fish products. Pregnant women are more susceptible to infection and this can result in miscarriage. Listeria will be killed during the correct cooking of non-ready to eat foods.
• In addition to being at increased risk from most food-poisoning bacteria, children seem to be particularly at risk of severe complications following STEC infection – including kidney failure and death.
• Guidance provided by relevant public health and food safety authorities on prevention of parasitic infection, as well as fermentation technologies and 'sear and shave' procedures, has been provided within this book.
• Curing salts must be measured accurately and used according to the manufacturer's instructions.
• Good hygiene practices during slaughter, distribution, butchery and preparation of meats that are cured without further cooking is essential to reduce the risk of contamination of finished products with harmful microorganisms.

For the reasons set out above, and to the fullest extent permitted by law, the author and publisher (i) cannot and do not accept any legal duty of care or responsibility in relation to the accuracy or appropriateness of the contents of this book, even where expressed as 'advice' or using other words to this effect, and (ii) disclaim any liability, loss, damage or risk that may be claimed or incurred as a consequence – directly or indirectly – of the use and/or application of any of the contents of this book.

This edition is published by Lorenz Books
an imprint of Anness Publishing Ltd
info@anness.com
www.lorenzbooks.com
www.annesspublishing.com

© Anness Publishing Ltd 2020

With thanks to Bianca & Mora, Exquisite Deli, The French Comte, Gastronomica, The Ham & Cheese Company.

Publisher: Joanna Lorenz
Photography: William Shaw
Props: Pene Parker
Design: Simon Daley
Index: Marie Lorimer